Full Hands, Full Heart, Full Circle

From New Mom to "Just Like You, Mom"

CATHY CARMODE LIM

ANN McDERMOTT PRESS

ANNISTON, ALABAMA

Library of Congress Control Number: 2005902293

ISBN: 0-9766888-4-0

Published by Ann McDermott Press
Anniston, AL 36207
Printed in the United States of America

To my mother, Carol Cromer, for being the mom I could
pattern myself after;
To my husband, Marce, for believing in dreams,
And to our daughters, Brianna, Marissa, and Camille –
words cannot capture my pride and awe

CONTENTS

FULL HANDS,
FULL HEART,
FULL CIRCLE

PART I
FULL OF DOUBTS

CHAPTER 1
THE SCARIEST ROLLER COASTER EVER:
THE METAMORPHOSIS

A full-length mirror used to hang on the back of my bed-room door. Now all that remain on that door are four metal hooks forming a rectangle. My husband has asked if I'd like another one. Sure, I would, but I don't see the point. Eventually, on one of those really bad days, it would go the way of the original. So I've just been content seeing my torso and most of my legs reflected in the shorter glass which, thanks to its location on my armoire, won't bring me bad luck for the next seven years.

I thank my children for that amputated view of myself. Were it not for their antics, I wouldn't continue to hear those four hooks swinging and scraping against my door as it slams shut with me inside, shaking like I did in the delivery room, post-epidural and pre-pushing, and questioning my sanity for having gone ahead and pushed.

Don't get me wrong. I love being a mother. But it's the hardest job I've ever had, among the variety that now innocuously populate the black-and-white page of my rarely used résumé. I didn't enter my current profession lightly or with rose-colored glasses. I knew I was in for a hard, long haul — the long part would be about twenty-five years, probably, and the hard ... well, you just don't know until you live it.

I wasn't the type of girl who grew up dreaming of getting married and having babies. I didn't own many dolls, and my sister and brother were respectively two and five years younger, so I wasn't exactly their caretaker when they were infants. I had two cousins who were a little younger, but whom I saw only twice a year, so I didn't cut my teeth on childcare that way either. And I sure didn't go looking for outside work as a baby sitter. On the occasions I was assessed by some adult to be a good match for their little ones, I reluctantly went along, but the two or three hours I did sit were endless and felt like slave labor for the small pittance I earned. I didn't advertise my services and was happy that few people assumed I would like to sit just because I was "that age."

When I married at age twenty-three, I knew I wasn't ready for babies immediately. Of course I wanted them — because it was expected culturally, because I did want to have a happy family unit, because I wouldn't have envisioned a life without them. Children were part of the master plan, somewhere in my future as an adult.

Then it just seemed to be time, somehow. Time to be an adult (or at least play the part because I was way past the magic ages of eighteen and twenty-one), time to make our family of two into a family of three. Surely it couldn't be that huge of an adjustment, having a tiny person around. Everyone else did it and surely so could I.

I found out very quickly "adjustment" is utterly the wrong word to use in describing that metamorphosis from carefree young woman (one, for instance, who can dash off to the mall whenever there's a spare hour, toting only a small purse, and try on ten pairs of shoes, or go to Washington, D.C., alone for a week to slowly and methodically explore every display in the National Gallery of Art) to "mom," who can only go to the mall after getting prepared with stroller, diaper bag, treats and toys, and psyched up to deal with a slew of whiny complaints. (And an art gallery? Ha. Does "bull in a china shop" sound like an apt description?)

It's like saying the scientist in the classic horror film "The Fly" went through an "adjustment" when his human cells were spliced, mixed and stirred with those of the winged, bazillion-eyed insect in his transporter machine, never to be set right again. He ended his wretched existence as some garden-variety spider's lunch.

My body, my mind, my mentality, my routine, my expectations were chopped up and stuck in a blender, never to be solid again. I was taken completely off guard. Sure, I had heard — as most women expecting their first child hear along with all that unsolicited advice — motherhood is an adjustment; life will never be the same again; yada, yada, yada. I got all that advice from friends, acquaintances, old ladies, young ladies, a cashier across the counter at the McDonald's where I had to have yet another orange drink (who also had the temerity to comment that I looked big enough to be having twins — a smart thing to say to a sensitive woman swimming in hormones and lugging around a full-grown baby in her stretched-to-the-limit midsection). So I knew, theoretically, that motherhood would mean some changes in my life.

But I had no idea what change felt like until I gave birth. Becoming a mother sent me spinning, knocked me into that sci-fi universe where everything looks the same but is really the anti-matter version of what we know in this world. Compounding the challenge of that change was the unexpect-

edness of its pure, undiluted concentration, as well as having
as a sick sense of isolation, of being a pariah among parents.
This because as I looked around at other glowing madonnas,
I couldn't see that they were sinking just as surely as I was in
that strongly brewed amniotic fluid. Only later would I learn
that many shared the ambivalence, doubts, frustrations, even
resentment — and, most of all, the guilt for feeling all of the
above — about their cherubic little gifts from "a Bob," as one
of my kids' books jokes.

It took me a solid year to slowly "adjust" to my new and
completely foreign reality, what boiled down to the utter lack
of personal time and space inherent in being a mom. I had
been so independent, so ferocious about making my own decisions, about having "me" time, about knowing what I wanted
and working toward it. Now, I was tethered to a helpless infant
by my nipples every hour or two, day in, day out. The
moment I finally lay down to rest, I had to pop back up again
with a start at the sound of a reedy but insistent cry. I was
needed every other minute of the day for diaper changes, for
comfort, for rocking, for sleep-inducing, for play. Even if I had
baby-sat more, and liked it, I couldn't have been prepared for
this metamorphosis.

When my daughter grew older and less dependent on me
specifically and bigger people in general, I felt a little less tethered and a little more free, like myself again, like maybe I
could occasionally just dash off to the mall to try on a succes-
sion of dresses (all a couple of sizes bigger than before). But
then I quit my part-time job when she was a year old to be a
stay-at-home mother, a recalibration that took six to twelve
months. Next (my friends and I all say we have to be a little
crazy to try pregnancy multiple times), I took the leap to con-
ceive again, after which I moved cross-country and had my

second baby two weeks after moving into my new house. At least the second time around, I didn't have to adjust to the actual state of motherhood. Thank heavens, the first child seems to take care of that. But I did have to adjust to having *two* little people demanding my time, which seemed to buck the laws of mathematics, two times the number of children adding up to far more than double the demands of just one.

In analyzing how I could have become so shell-shocked, I realize I expected my life would stay the same, that *I* would fundamentally stay the same, except that my routines would change slightly, that I would just have to *do* some more things than I did before. But I was wrong, wrong, wrong. My life is not the same at all. I'm not the same at all. It's not a difference in scheduling, in getting used to less sleep and more laundry. It's a whole change in outlook, in attitude, in perception of life itself. And I think I can generally say that is mostly for the better. I'm a better person. I'm a little more patient, a little more grounded, a little less selfish.

But the biggest difference of all is how much more full and complete (not perfectly so, mind you, but further along the continuum) my life is today, a few years into my life in this oddly similar yet foreign anti-matter world. At any date B.C. (Before Children), there was me, my husband, my work, my hobbies and other obligations. Now I have all that plus my miraculous, unique, raven-haired little wonders who make me laugh, cry, giggle, scream, grin unbearably, see life differently. They take up all my time, they make me crazy and angry and frustrated enough that I will never be able to see my whole body reflected in a full-length mirror, but sometimes I'm able to step away from it and see the real me, rather than just the image in the glass of an armoire.

That real me, post children, is much more complex and

crazy than I could ever have imagined I would be. Imagination only ventures so far.

As I have learned through experience, being a mother could be likened to having multiple personalities or being manic-depressive. It's a roller-coaster ride on the grandest scale, of dizzying emotions that carry a woman way up into the clouds and then sweep her way back down to hover just above the littered dirt ground that holds up the tracks. As she falls almost straight down, any typical mom will feel the anger, frustration, doubt, isolation, and complete inadequacy that taunts mothers who want the best for their children — and who know at that same instant and all other instants in time that they're not it.

Moms race along, being bumped and jostled by nagging feelings of self-doubt just as roughly as old wooden coasters throw one about, through small and large hills. The bumps remind them, "You're never going to get this right. You're always going to make mistakes. Your constant missteps — the yelling, the impatience, the missed opportunities for teaching and gentle interaction — will put your kids in therapy for half their adulthood."

No matter what, go the screams along the coaster, you're going to screw up your children. Either way you'll be wrong. If you yell at them at all, they'll be damaged psychologically. If you don't discipline them, they'll be spoiled. If you work outside the home, if you pursue any personal dreams even if you stay at home, somehow that surely will take away from the needs of your children. But if you don't dare to dream something just for yourself, you'll die inside and your children will have a hollow imitation of a parent. It's a constant battle with the competing voices in your head.

But then the roller coaster sweeps the manic mom back

up. She sees the bright blue hue of the sky, adorned with puffy white cotton-ball clouds fashioned by sticky, chubby hands. She feels during those sunny moments in the sky that all is perfectly right with her world. Her children are beautiful, happy and amazing; she is fulfilled just being their caretaker and having the exquisite gift of watching them grow and learn and explore. The joy in just having had that opportunity to give birth and see a new and entirely unique life come into its own is all-encompassing.

And the ride goes down and around again, small loops and hills intermixed with tall screaming heights. I never would have imagined how difficult it would be day to day to maintain some semblance of equilibrium — to hold on to my lunch. I still have no idea if it will ever end, if I can get off the ride and collapse for a blissful retirement in a sunny park with cool shade trees and fountains, populated by happy and giggling grandchildren racing through the clearing on occasion. As I ride my coaster around and around now, my young children keeping me crazy, I am not completely sure if when I get to that peaceful park, I will be able to sit back and relax, reflecting with satisfaction on the sum of the ride, or if nagging doubts will tarnish my reveries.

Sometimes, however, I glance in that mirror, step back and think. I get the feeling, given the ways I've stretched and changed so far on this roller coaster, that I will by then have grown enough through it all to be able to pat myself on the back for a job pretty well done, for a ride endured and enjoyed, and above all, for children who have not only survived my parenting but thrived and grown into reasonably adjusted adults, unique, happy, and prepared for their own crazy rides into adulthood and motherhood. Yes, the lows were very low, but the highs and even the whole nutty, noisy experience were so richly satisfying I would have regretted staying on solid ground.

I'll treasure all the moments we're making day to day as mom and daughters, since that's what mothering — and life — are all about. A sum of suspended moments, some of them jam-packed with joy, some spiked with tension and impatience, some just right at the fill line of peace and contentment. The beauty of the moments is that they are both completely unique and at the very same time stunningly reminiscent of perfect past moments. They bring to mind spiritually familiar emotions, ageless feelings that seem to have been experienced in past lives, the details of which are forgotten, but the imprints of which are permanent. That sense of déjà vu is one that is the most comforting of all; it seems to say at each juncture that the moment was meant to be, that it was planned all along to add its own color to the grand tapestry of life. For what seems like good or ill, it all adds up to something that is glorious and rich.

Those moments as a mom give me light and hope and tell me that I am doing something right, that I'm filling a role intended for me. They make me realize that I'm one in a line of mothers who have struggled and strained and loved and triumphed. And that my own daughters will take their place in that line and will struggle and strain and triumph just as I and my mother and her mother have done. Here I share a few of these moments, both the highs and the lows, and just a glimpse of the interconnections between them.

CHAPTER 2
LEARNING CURVE AHEAD

The first few weeks after giving birth to Brianna, I wasn't immediately immersed in maternal milky feelings and sheer love for my newborn. I didn't feel instantly like a mother, as if the oxytocin washing over me should transform me into a different person than I was before I saw two pink lines on a pregnancy test. I didn't spend all my time gazing dreamily at my tiny bundle of joy, feeding and bathing her reverently, the two of us a little island to ourselves. I guess I didn't get the special shot at the hospital (maybe they left it out of that blessed compound of medicines that flows in the epidural), or that new-mother kit containing free diaper, ointment and wipe samples was missing an easy-open plastic packet of attachment serum. I just wasn't experiencing what I had read or heard about in popular literature and culture. It made me more than a little uneasy that after leaping into this huge commitment I could very well never get the hang of it.

Contrary to what I thought all other new moms were experiencing, I was walking around in a fog, tired, bloated, hugely overweight and unable to wear anything but maternity clothes. No brilliant ideas for handling this alien seven-pound crying machine penetrated the fog that encased me mentally as solidly as a new layer of fat enrobed me physically. I desperately wanted to get back into a normal routine — *any* routine at all. I wanted to sit down to eat a meal in peace, and be able to prepare it without having to rig my daughter into the Snugli as I (unsuccessfully) attempted to stir and chop; I wanted to be able to put her down to go to the bathroom or to shower without her tiny face wrinkling up instantaneously in a primal scream of abandonment. I was an amateur trying to perform delicate brain surgery and I couldn't even figure out whether to cut the scalp or the soles of the feet. As I look back at pictures of myself during that time, the lost and bewildered look on my face takes me right back to the helplessness that permeated my being.

To add insult to injury, Brianna couldn't *do* anything, making her not much company but a whole heck of a lot of work. For a few weeks, she didn't smile except for some grimaces during diaper activity; she couldn't wave or make really cute faces yet; she couldn't talk to me, even to say "no" yet; she was just a very small and demanding bundle of open mouth and flailing limbs, arms that jerked in reflex when startled and cleverly got right in the way of a bulb syringe, and legs that kicked around enough to make it an Olympic event to fasten a diaper. So far, the motherhood gig wasn't all it was cracked up to be.

But very slowly, as I began acclimating to the foreign land in which sleep, energy and free time were just as much in scarce supply as oxygen at the top of Mt. Everest, and as Brianna began growing and doing new things, I started getting excited about the little skills she was learning. When she truly smiled at me for the first time, a little shiver of happiness ran up my spine. I felt a little connection, that she recognized me as her mother and was grateful for my efforts. When she rolled over, I was amazed at the strength and determination she displayed, with all the little steps it took for her to figure out how to maneuver herself from one side to the other. As she began interacting with me, I started to see her personality emerge — her intelligence, her vitality, her energy.

As she gets older year by year and day by day, she continues to amaze me. As I began noticing and writing down all these stupendous feats of hers, Brianna had progressed to a mature and very articulate and garrulous age three, and was much smarter than I would have guessed someone her age would be. (But what do I know? I had nothing to compare her with.)

One day early in that time, we were reading the "book of the week" (the one of only two she insisted on reading every day, naptime and bedtime, over and over), which was the "Little Counting Book." On one page, there are five race cars, each labeled with a number from one to five. I asked Brianna to count the race cars because I knew she could count to five. But as she pointed to the race cars one by one, instead of simply tallying them and ignoring the number branded on the side of each vehicle, she proceeded clockwise and told me the numbers on the cars, so it ended up sounding like this: "One, two, five, four, three." I was astounded. She was *reading* the numbers! Duly impressed, perhaps only as a mother can be, I burst out in awe, "Good *job,* Brianna!" She cheerily but matter-of-factly replied, "Thank you," seemingly oblivious to her big accomplishment, and we continued to read the book.

My maternal pride was really kicking in, in retrospect a good sign that I am making progress toward my motherhood degree (don't ask me when I get the diploma). On another occasion, I purchased a Father's Day card and asked Brianna to draw a little on it, in lieu of a signature. I handed her the card and a pen and went about my business. A few minutes later, she piped up, "Look, Mom, a *T*!" and then "Look, an *O*!" I glanced over at her workmanship, wondering if she was just fancying herself to have drawn some letters, and sure enough, I found a *T* and an *O* written a little shakily but undeniably on the paper, next to a few standard stick figures. I was dumbfounded, once again. I had not tried to show her how to write at all; no lessons on forming letters, no push to be a writer. We had just read books, with me casually pointing out letters and asking her what they were. And here out of the clear blue sky (or pen), she had started writing all on her own. Wow. I was almost speechless, but I found the words to tell her, "Yes, Brianna, that sure is an *O* and *T*! Good job!"

More recently, my newfound maternal pride has taken note of what I consider to be promising artistic talent. Brianna draws some funny pictures of Daddy, Mommy and herself and a few other stray characters. Her sticks have grown a little more sophisticated, and she's added buildings and trees and so on. She's also gotten pretty adept at coloring within the lines in coloring books. My husband and I both think this is impressive, almost precocious, like she's a prodigy on her way to becoming the next Picasso.

With each new day and each new gift I see in Brianna, I praise her warmly but sincerely. My feelings and encouraging comments are not forced feedback or some program of "positive reinforcement" that some child-rearing experts tell me to incorporate into my treatment of my children. My praise is genuine, from my heart. I know it makes her happy by the way she responds with an enthusiastic but simple "thank you." I can see that my daily affirmations of admiration for her have a very positive cumulative effect, for she is happy and pleasant and content with herself.

She isn't afraid to try new things, seemingly confident that she will succeed, at least in having tried and made some progress.

I can't help but think of my own childhood and the way my parents acted with me. They consistently, genuinely praised my efforts all along, giving me wonderful support in my schoolwork, in my voluminous extracurricular activities and varied interests. They took me to lessons in piano or dance or gymnastics and came to recitals and awards ceremonies. They occasionally treated me to dinner or some other goodie when I reached a milestone or achieved an important goal. They just told me that I was smart, that they had confidence in me, that they knew I could do it, and I usually did. I have generally had the feeling that I can try anything I am interested in and that I have a decent chance of succeeding. Their consistent, real confidence in me and their parental amazement by my abilities shored me up and made me feel valued and capable. Even now, my mom reads the snippets from this book and makes specific comments about why she likes it so much. She tells me she knows I'm going to make it.

My husband has gotten in on the act of genuine support, as well. He reads and re-reads everything I write. I catch him late at night, between games of computer Solitaire or Tetris, poring over sections he's read ten times already. I know he believes in me and that he must really like what I've done. It makes me feel happy and supported, sure of succeeding.

Even Brianna gives back a little of that same confidence I have in her. She praises me when I do something to her liking, such as when I make a good dinner or fix a broken toy. "Good JOB, Mommy!" she enthusiastically says, giving me a sage smile and almost a wink. She makes me happy too. Those bits of sincere praise reciprocated from my once-helpless infant go a long way to making me feel not so helpless as a mother, after all.

CHAPTER 3
PERCEIVING THE POSITIVE

The really good moments in which I feel encouraged in my skills as a mom seem to come after the really bad moments in which I feel there's no way I should ever have had sex, period, let alone with the express purpose of having offspring. What could I have been thinking? Surely someone is going to find out about my lack of skills and cart me away.

There are plenty of occasions for frustration, too. One day was pretty typical: one of those child-rearing days in which everything external seems to go wrong and everything internal too, one in which the child absolutely will not *cooperate*. I foolishly attempted to shop at the mall and elsewhere in the big city an hour away, toting my impatient children with me. Children do NOT like errand-running, particularly in a strange place. All the fruit snacks, crackers, and juice in the world (or in the small diaper bag) could not have kept them happy. I should probably have stayed home, shut the girls in their room supplied with a few boxes full of toys, and just let them destroy the place and clean up later. But by golly, I wanted to actually get some things DONE, for a change, and I threw caution and common sense to the wind.

I paid the price, believe me. They fussed the whole time, every stop we made, in and out of the car, in and out of strollers, in and out of shopping carts. There were moments I fantasized just a little bit about accidentally leaving them in a cart to let a kindly grandmotherly type wrap them up and take them home, like irresistibly cute stray kittens.

As is the case with such evenings that come at the end of such eternal, excruciatingly trying days, I gladly would have bypassed the nightly bedtime reading routine with Brianna because my energy/patience/love bank was overdrawn, but I knew from experience that wasn't an option. It's hard enough to get her to wind down and go to sleep when the routine is perfectly executed; it's nearly impossible if the ritual isn't followed to the letter. So I sucked in my accumulated day's stress, put on a brave face, and we read as always.

But somehow this time, instead of feeding on my stress and sending it back to me amplified as only a three-year-old can (I think they know how close you are to going berserk and they relish witnessing the drama of it just like spectators at a bullfight), Brianna was in high charm gear; her every word and look was endearing and absolutely devoid of preschooler attitude. Reading this evening seemed a relief, even a source of income for my patience bank, instead of a depleting chore. We both enjoyed ourselves.

After the books had been put away, I leaned over to Brianna for the usual kiss and hug. I looked at her and saw the sweet look of innocence and love in her face and melted even more. I held her tight and whispered that I loved her very much. She leaned in close and gazed deeply into my eyes, seeing through them and into my heart. She kept looking, focusing on one of my eyes, and it was then that I knew at least one big part of what held her gaze. She said with an air of fascination and wonder, "I can see myself in your eyes!"

On the surface, I knew she saw her reflection on the glossy

surface of my irises. My eyes and hers are both deep brown, a very dark color that makes for good mirroring. My husband has dark eyes and hair, naturally, being Filipino, and we have always jokingly battled over which of us has the darker eyes. Although I am blonde and fairer of skin, I have almost black-ly brown eyes, and I tease him that his basic browns pale next to mine. Regardless of which of us is right and wins the con-test of brownest parental eye coloring, Brianna won the child — and even family — division. Her eyes are like warm, high-ly glossed mahogany, reflecting everything back to the atten-tive viewer. As I looked closer at her while she stayed focused on my right eye, I could see in her eyes my slightly distorted face staring back at me.

My tiny funhouse-mirror eyes distorted her face crazily for her just as I saw my visage grown fat in the middle from the concave curve of her eyes. But for the few moments she intently bored a hole into my eyeball, her gaze went deeper, and she saw more. What she was thinking is what intrigues me. The questions flew through my mind later as I reflected on those freeze-framed moments.

Did she see my feelings at that moment or the feelings of the day? Was she reminded of the poor example I had set for her that day as I had lost my cool trying to pack too much into one trip to the city? I hoped she wouldn't remember how I had acted under the pressure, and I hoped even more that she wouldn't unconsciously act that way herself later on in life. Could she sense my feelings of inadequacy as I struggle day to day to face and overcome the weaknesses that are sometimes so obvious?

I want my daughters to grow up feeling loved, cherished and special, but it's sometimes difficult to give that gift to them when my deeply-entrenched feelings of insecurity (not just as a mother but as a woman, as a writer, as a person) make me feel far less than special and undeserving of being loved and cherished myself.

Could Brianna perceive that I want to be the mother she deserves but that I often feel that I'm not up to the challenge? This is the hardest job I've ever taken on in my life, and on my bad days I fear I'd get fired if it were the nine-to-five kind of career (there are definitely times I need a vacation, but never do I want to change careers). But I keep pushing on, doing my best, hoping that she remembers my best days, the days where I teach her how to handle challenges properly and the days on which I just show her I love her by my every action. I hope she saw in my eyes the regret for the lessons yet unlearned and my sincere desire to learn those lessons soon so she can learn them from me.

Did she see more than just her distorted face reflected in my eyes, but also her soul, her best inner qualities? Did she envision the lovable, miraculous creature that I saw? Locked in a silent exchange of understanding with my daughter, I forgot the blunders of my day and my insecurities and focused instead on this growing personality who had started as just a tiny cluster of chromosomes deep within my own body. Brianna had matured in a few short years from an utterly dependent extension of myself to a fairly independent, unique being who was capable of reaching into my soul and teaching me lessons I never dreamed of learning. She was showing me daily her capabilities for creativity, wisdom, growth and love, and I was seeing them clearly all at once as we shared this moment.

I hope she saw that. I hope she doesn't take as her inheritance from me an ability to see the negative qualities in one-self and ignore the mountains of positive traits, but that she is able to see and remember these moments in which I saw all the best in her.

I hope that she truly saw herself — her whole self — reflected in my eyes, for I saw it clearly. And it was beautiful, miraculous, and holy. I saw hope, love, and boundless possibilities for the future — for her and for me both.

PART II
FULL HANDS

CHAPTER 4
I NEED MY SPACE

If I had a quarter for every time I've heard "Boy, you've got your hands full!" from some stranger who thinks they're being clever or commiserating or funny, I could fill up my house with stacks of those cardboard collectors' displays of the fifty special-edition state coins my husband is trying to amass. (Scene: the movie theater: I hand the cashier a number of bills and three coins. "Hey wait! Lemme look at those quarters. Aww, already got a few Connecticuts.") Then I could fill up another house with tiny but weighty plastic canisters, once holding film destined to shoot endless likenesses of our breathtakingly photogenic children but now turned into my husband's piggy banks. I hear it all the time. Needless to say, the sheen of that probably never-funny statement wore off hundreds of thousands of utterings ago.

Yes, I *do* have my hands full. I only have two of them at this point (maybe someday that genetic mapping research will lead to more appendages for moms), and that's barely a suitable number of limbs for taking care of a house *or* taking care of one child *or* writing and editing. Throw all of it in the mix with two needy little stinkers and you've got a major shortage of appendages. Whatever happened to supply and demand?

Parenting young children is challenging. It is an endless stream of diapers and demands, feeding and cleaning up. It means constant vigilance. Babies need food and fresh bottoms when they're awake. Toddlers need stimuli. Children who can talk churn out questions that beg answering.

There are the tough or scientific queries like "Why is the sky blue?" and "Where do babies come from?", but more common and constant are the all-purpose "What is that?" and "What are you doing?" as running commentary on whatever happens to be going on. Typically, the latter two questions are asked about five hundred times every day, cycling over and over. Day after day, I feel caught in some freaky space-time-loop like Bill Murray in *Groundhog Day*.

My responses are usually obvious answers like "I'm cooking an egg" or "I'm putting on makeup" or "I'm getting a shower — put the curtain down! &*@$ – get a towel for that puddle" and, several times a day, "I'm going potty. *Close the door!*" Occasionally as a new day dawns, Brianna catches on, moving from query to simple observation: "You're putting on makeup?" Or "You're going potty?" I must admit that I quickly tire of so many questions. I'm sometimes relieved to hear just that statement of fact coming out of her mouth, minus the traditional higher-pitched sound that accompanies the last few words before a question mark.

But even as I feel a general reticence (stemming largely from being overworked and overtired) to keep answering questions, which are thrown at me like baseballs in a batting cage by the best little question-pitcher in the minor leagues (during a fifty-nine-inning game with no seventh-inning stretch), I remind myself that questions are how my blossoming genius is learning. And she depends almost wholly on my knowledge and my willingness to impart that knowledge to her. At Brianna's tender age, Mommy is the source of all wisdom and information about the world at large and life in general (yikes!). Perhaps I should just enjoy the feeling of power that comes with my omniscient position for a little while instead of feeling annoyed and overworked by her constant search for greater understanding of the universe — since heaven knows that opinion will change by the time she hits adolescence. By then omniscient Mommy will be replaced by clueless Mom. Hm, this age is looking more appealing.

It's not just the deluge of questions or the running commentary on my daily activities that gets annoying; it's the fact that my child is old enough now that I'd better be prepared to include her in those daily activities, or curtail them in her presence altogether.

My parents' response to certain of these activities was to tell me "RHIP: Rank has its privileges!" when I complained that they got to do things they wouldn't let me do. They had acquired a certain set of rights and privileges to go along with their age and status as responsible parents, they were telling me. Implicit (or sometimes explicit) in these replies to my youthful whining were the concepts that I was young and hadn't acquired these privileges yet but that one day I would climb through the ranks and reach their high and mighty status too. So as I grew older and left home, I began enjoying the simple privileges that went along with age and rank. I ate what I want, when I wanted, and slept when I wanted and bought what I wanted.

Of course, what usually entailed "what I wanted" was pretty much the same things I had done before I acquired my independent rank and status. When I went to college, I still ate healthy foods, three good meals a day. I went to bed by 10 P.M. weeknights so I could wake up for 8 A.M. classes and function coherently. I only had a little bit of spending money, so buying what I wanted usually entailed a few new clothes on sale here and there and a milkshake at the many available purveyors of very thick frozen confections on and around campus. When I got married and finished college, my spending grew a bit as I earned money, so I spent it on bills, food, clothes, gadgets and electronics for our new apartment. I didn't spend, eat, or sleep out of bounds, but I enjoyed more power and autonomy than I had as a dependent at home.

But the one thing that I appreciated most the moment I left home and that I still relish eleven years later as a married mother of two is the delectable freedom — the absolutely unchecked hedonism — to open up my freezer at the end of the day, dish out as many scoops of ice cream as I'm willing to see pad my hips, and relish bite by bite in heavenly peace on my sofa. I know my parents had a similar habit. We always had ice cream in our freezer (actually, to be completely accurate, ice milk, always plain vanilla), and we children usually had a crack at it about once a week, but I know my mom and dad had it more often than that. Now I'm reveling in the privileges of rank. Ha! I earned it!

But now as I stand in my parents' higher-ranking shoes, I have children watching me.

I've learned by experience it's foolhardy to partake of ice cream before my little ones are safely tucked away in bed, walls and doors shielding their eyes from the enchanted glow of my tempting non-vanilla treat. However, when I succumb to my freezer's siren call before bedtime, Brianna attaches herself to me like a garrulous leech, pleading for bite after bite before I can get a spoonful to my own mouth, asking for more than I care to part with. When not satisfied with the frequency or volume of my handouts, she asks for some in her own bowl to eat at the table. Her request often melts my reservations; for one, the dessert is milk-based and reasonably healthy for a sweet, so I don't feel too guilty about her having some; second and more significantly, when she's busy with a bowl, I'm free to eat mine in peace.

Nutrition concerns aside, I have noticed one major drawback to giving my daughter ice cream during my personal evening winding-down routine: further restrictions on my freedom to partake as I prefer. Brianna turns into the food police. After she goes to the table (where we have made clear she is supposed to eat), I go my separate way to my familiar ice-cream-eating haunt curled up on the sofa, and Brianna takes notice of my conspicuous absence from the table.

"Mom, sit at the table!" comes the chirpy but authoritative command from the dining room. "You're supposed to eat at the table." She doesn't give up, either, and I'm forced to forsake my comfy sofa and sit down facing her on a hard dining-room chair, TV screen out of sight behind my back. It just isn't fair. Here I am, a full-fledged adult, and because I'm making the mistake of not waiting to eat my treat until after bedtime, I get relegated to the table. But I can't argue — Brianna's not old enough to understand the meaning of the old "RHIP," so I have to set a good example and follow the rules that I've set down for her.

It seems an eagle has built a nice, cozy nest in my house.

Brianna sees all and hears all; she doesn't miss a thing. If I slip up, if I don't do the things I've asked her to do, or if I do something I don't want her to see, she'll call me on it. Having a child is a sure way to quit swearing. I have never been one to use much bad language, but I've let a few slip in the past. I also use some phrases that seem to be OK coming out of my mouth, but if repeated, sound pretty questionable coming from a three-year-old. I've had to curtail the slightest negative speech patterns because I get them right back from my daughter. Believe me, as with eating at the table, there's no telling my daughter that I am an exception to the rule. I think in a few more years she'll be discerning enough that we can part ways a bit, but for now, if I want her to do it, I need to do it too. "Do as I say and not as I do" doesn't fly with anyone, especially not a teenager or a toddler.

So stuff I say to my daughter is coming back to haunt me, be it my injunctions for her to do something a certain way, to behave or be polite, or, on the other hand, my little slips of the tongue I don't want her to copy. She picks up on all of it. So I'm finding I have to obey my own rules, whether they're ones I've spelled out for her along the way or ones I haven't, guidelines that I set for myself that I have yet to obey perfectly. Invariably, these inner guidelines for myself are ways of living I hope my daughter can learn just by following my good example. Having her around gives me more incentive to do better. Maybe she will grow up naturally and automatically practicing good habits without struggling to learn them when she's older and more set in her ways. Maybe she won't have to unlearn some bad habits, bad behaviors, the way I have. One can hope.

Lately, unfortunately, it seems, I'm getting an earful of reminders from Brianna about speaking quietly, not reacting too passionately. I think she's inherited my (and my family's) ability to be a little dramatic, to fervently broadcast on a high frequency our displeasure or frustration with given hiccups in our lives. I've told her more than a few times to calm down, not to whine or fuss, not to overreact. Now it's coming right back, like a little tape recording, at the most inopportune times. "Calm down!" "Don't whine!" I'm already coming unhinged; hearing a rebuke from a three-foot-tall upstart makes me want to whip around and smack her impudent little butt (a mere fantasy, a checked urge, but enticing nonetheless).

I have been working on this for a while myself, trying to get myself to chill out about perceived stresses that just aren't that big of a deal in the grand scheme of things. I constantly tell myself to "Calm down." Just take it easy, don't worry about it; it's not a big deal. As my mother has put it in our many lengthy phone discussions, "Is it going to kill you? If not, then it's not worth worrying so much about." I try to de-stress and calm down and relax: not get angry, not get frustrated, not lash out at innocent parties around me. I've become moderately successful at this little technique. But up until now, I've been accepting of hearing my own recorded message in my own voice playing reminders in my head.

Hearing it in stereo from an outside source, and a three-year-old at that, is a little annoying. I could kick myself for ever having said anything to her in the first place. But it sure is sobering, humbling, and motivational. The better my own inner recording gets at modifying my less-than-best behavior, the less I'll hear my daughter flick on her recording, and — one would hope — the less she will end up having to do it for herself when she gets old like me.

However, even as I am reminded (sometimes daily) of my imperfections by the eagle-eyed observations of my daughter, I am equally reminded of my strengths, the lessons I have successfully taught her by word and deed that are good, pure, and noble.

Brianna has learned to be polite. From the very beginnings

of her language formation, my husband and I told her to say "please," "thank you," "you're welcome" and "excuse me," among other niceties. We instructed her what to say when, and reminded her each time the opportunity arose. If she asked for (or demanded) a cracker or a glass of water, we let her know that she wouldn't get it until she asked the nice way.

What's more, we didn't just tell her she needed to do this, we spoke politely ourselves. We say "please" and "thank you" when we speak to each other as parents, and we are polite in kind to Brianna. I feel sure she wouldn't take us seriously if we simply expected her to use mannerly language with us while neglecting to do so ourselves. So now Brianna is a very polite little girl. She usually employs proper language and kind words with us and with anyone she meets, enough that she draws praise from other adults for her good behavior. I'm appreciative that my parents taught me how to be polite so that I could easily pass it on to my daughters.

Every day I hear "I love you, Mom." I get hugs and kisses. I see a sweet little child who truly loves me and wants to learn from me, who is eager to follow in my footsteps. I see her share her toys, hug her little sister. I feel awash in warm gratitude for the little gifts that are in my life. I must be doing something right, because I truly love my girl and tell her that every day. I must be practicing what I preach when it comes to the love I feel for her.

CHAPTER 5
I NEED A NAP

Parenting books, magazines and newspaper columns, as well as fellow parents, are chock-full of advice on how to discipline and rear a child so that he or she will grow to maturity being responsible, hard-working, and good, and so that the youngster will live in such a way that the parents don't completely pull out all of their hair and/or leave the child (usually a two- or three-year-old) on a kindly stranger's doorstep. For those of you who may be unaware of this fact (and who obviously, then, haven't been blessed with the gift of toddlers), raising small children is *very difficult* some days, and definitely the hardest job you will ever do (let's not even talk about adolescents). I would probably have a lower blood pressure and stress level working the floor of the New York Stock Exchange compared with some days parenting Brianna.

So I'm always in need of a break from my high-stress job. I don't know much about those brokers on the NYSE floor, but most likely they get lunch and coffee breaks. That's federally mandated, right? Workers get breaks. But in parenting, the hardest work ever, breaks are not mandated or mentioned. The two things I look forward to most in my day are related in that they give me some length of a break: one, the arrival of my husband home from work, and two, naptime. Having an alternate caretaker in the form of a person or a state of unconsciousness gives me an opportunity to sit down, rest a bit, gather my thoughts, focus for a few minutes on remedial personal hygiene, and maybe even read, sleep, or write.

My husband's arrival from work is guaranteed and requires no effort on my part but waiting (and patience, elusive as it is, is a virtue I am being forced to acquire). Naptime, however, is another matter. It's a daily struggle. I've heard that sticking to the same routine every day helps, but it's no guarantee. In my experience, it gives some good structure and lets Brianna know what to expect, but it doesn't prevent her from fighting it frequently.

What usually happens at my dreaded hour of 1 to 2 p.m. is at the very least some half-hearted but short-lived muttering and foot-dragging and at the worst an escalation of the mumbling and reluctance into an award-winning performance complete with enough thrashing around, yelling, screaming and crying to land my poor wide-awake daughter in her room for long enough that the solitary confinement turns into a nap anyway. Most often, the conversation goes something like this:

"Brianna, it's time to take a nap." (I patiently, firmly and hopefully state in a matter-of-fact parental voice.)

"I don't WANNA take a nap!!" (*Whining*)

"I understand that, but it is time. Let's read a book." (I try reasonably successfully to keep a patient tone in my firm voice.)

"I don't WANNA read a book!" (*More whining*)

"OK, then you can just go to sleep without reading a book." (The patient voice starts to get a small edge of exasperation.)

"I don't WANT to go to sleep!" (*Whining* ad nauseam)

"It's time. Let's read a book." (I go back to the simple fact, hopeful again.)

After this exchange, which probably happens every other day (some days are heaven-sent, during which she quietly and obediently sits down to read and sleep), we move on to the next phase, where we sit down on her bed and read three or four books, after which Brianna drinks some milk and requests her stuffed animals and blankets. After the animals are laid on the bed, in a very strict routine of two and then one and then two again, and the blankets are settled properly on top of her legs, Brianna generally acquiesces and lies quietly and sleeps. I may receive one or two callbacks from the door or hallway for extra hugs and kisses, but these tend to be proportional to how resistant she feels to taking the nap.

On the better days, the routine goes smoothly and I let out a sigh of relief and head to my bed or the couch, my freedom, my respite, my refuge. On the worst days, her digging in of heels, whether before or after the book-reading, can be the beginning of an hour or even two of stubborn refusal to lie down and allow eyelids to close. It's on these days that I find my patience as a mother being tested to its utter limit. Usually, I try to put Brianna down right after her baby sister goes to sleep, so they're both sleeping at the same time, so I can get some real time alone, in a quiet house.

Of course, I try to make sure that Brianna's heel-digging doesn't turn into enough noise to wake up her little sister. That would foil my plans. So I'm desperate. I'm tense. I'm exhausted. I sit in the living room, the opposite end of the house from where Brianna is resisting sleep, where there are two closed doors between us to muffle the din, and I breathe deeply a few times. I may turn on the television, catch up on some shows, turn up the volume just enough so it doesn't keep my children up but that it can drown out some of that three-year-old background noise. Or I might just lie there on the couch, taking cleansing breaths, slowing down my racing pulse and blood pressure. I wait and hope and pray for quiet.

On better days, perhaps when I'm at a satisfactory level of rest, patience, and energy, I reflect philosophically on the whole crazy situation. I almost — just almost — feel a little sorry for Brianna, that it's hard to sleep when other more interesting things beckon. I think back to my own childhood and to the mother who shepherded me through that childhood. Napping wasn't a favorite activity of mine as a child or even a teen, when some late nights would seemingly call for extra rest. My mother says ruefully that she never could get me to take naps; now I really feel sorry for her, too. I feel her pain.

I clearly remember lying on my bed once when I was about five or six, trying to be quiet for a while because my mother had ordered me to my room, with the door shut, to sleep for just an hour. She was in the living room and kitchen area, on the floor below my room, in an older house to boot, so I knew I had to try to be obedient since the floors were creaky. When I settled myself onto my nice big double bed at the beginning of my confinement, I hoped that despite my poor track record I would somehow be able to fall asleep, because if I didn't sleep, I'd be bored stiff lying there, just pretending.

When my hopes for a pass-the-time sleep were dashed, I lay as quietly and as still as possible for what seemed a good long while, hoping that my offering would appease my mother's demand. After what seemed an eternity in child-time, I got off my bed and tried to play very quietly and inconspicuously, still in my room with the door closed, until naptime was up. When I went downstairs later, Mom mentioned right away that she was on to my game: "I heard you up there. You didn't sleep at all." Busted! And I honestly had the best of intentions.

Back then, I didn't understand why in the world my mom would insist on my sleeping if I wasn't tired. What's the point of that? Obviously, now I know why she forced quiet time on me: *she* needed a break. And she wasn't too angry when I came down an hour later, never having slept. I am sure she was happy to have an hour with me out of her hair, whether it was a nap or Lincoln Logs that tied me up. (Although now that I think about it, what were my little brother – a baby – and sister – three years old – doing then? It's hard to imagine she accomplished the feat of having three children taking naps at the same time.)

My struggles with naps didn't end in childhood. I remember a couple of headaches I had while a teenager. For some reason, both occurred on vacation at my grandmother's house. I complained about my head hurting, so both my mom and grandma told me to take some aspirin and go to sleep. They told me if I went to sleep that it wouldn't hurt anymore — naturally, I wouldn't feel it when I was asleep, and then when I woke up it would be gone.

For the sake of the promised pain relief, I tried very hard to go to sleep. I lay on a twin bed in my grandma's guest room, staring up at the window shades I had drawn in a desperate attempt to make the room darker — anything to create an environment conducive to sleeping — hoping I would get to sleep soon so the pain would go away. Amazingly enough, I did manage to get to sleep on both of those occasions — and Mom and Grandma were right — I *did* feel better!

Mysteriously, as soon as I hit college, I began taking naps. I think I took them at least once a week, often once a day. All the hard work, walking to classes, staying up studying (or talking and goofing around with friends in the dorm) took its toll and converted me to napping. I was sold on the merits of daytime sleep. A good nap could cure anything.

Theoretically, I still think naps are great things. I am tired frequently — I have a three-year-old and an infant. (Case closed.) But I find it very difficult to take naps. Part of it is that it is challenging to find an opportunity to actually lie down and get the shuteye; both of my children don't always sleep at the same time during the day. But a bigger part of it is that when I do get the opportunity, on the days that the girls are sleeping at the same time, or when my husband is home and actively encouraging me to rest (I've observed, a bitter envy rising in my chest, that he has no trouble whatsoever dozing off instantaneously for three or thirty minutes, however long is available and however much he needs to recuperate), I just can't stand the thought of "wasting" my time sleeping. Time to myself is a precious commodity, more treasured than hefty bricks of gleaming gold; sleep ends up low on my list of things to do for myself. Theoretically, I know I need it, but practically, when push comes to shove, I can't shove myself into that cocoon of pillows and blankets to sleep.

Countless weekend afternoons come and go in which I am so exhausted that I can barely think clearly to get anything done. My husband, being the sensitive, giving soul he is, tells me to go rest; he'll watch the baby. But as soon as I lie down on my bed, I begin making shopping and to-do lists in my head. I concoct new ideas for books or articles. I think of birthday cards or gifts that must be bought and sent. I devise menus for the next week. In short, I can't fall asleep because I'm thinking of all the exciting things I have to do, just like Brianna. But as soon I throw aside the gift of naptime and get up to *do* something about all these things in my head, I can't do anything well because my body has run out of gas and my brain is enshrouded in fog.

Which brings me to a realization that makes me empathize with my daughter: Of course she doesn't want to lie down and sleep; that would mean going into a room alone, turning off the lights and abandoning her packed schedule of watching videos, reading, singing, analyzing little critters' daily schedules, and discovering new things to play with. What could be more boring and useless than a nap! How difficult it must be to lie down and rest when she knows how many interesting things are awaiting her outside the bounds of her mattress.

As much as I empathize with my daughter, however, many late afternoons of observation have led me to conclude that Brianna doesn't have my childhood "problem" of not being tired at naptime. She's fussy, cranky, frustrating — a big mess. She makes herself and all the rest of us miserable because she's overly tired. While she's too young to realize lack of rest is the problem, I know that when I force her to take a nap, two hours later she'll wake up and be in a wonderful, cheery, ready-to-explore-the-world-again mood. She can hop right back into her discovery routine and be perfectly pleasant to be around. And I can deal with her much more patiently and easily when she is not cranky and crying simply from being tired. So I go through the trouble of getting her down for a nap day after day because I know it will be worth it for both of us.

It takes a good day or a whole lot of cleansing breaths (or chocolate) for me to think back to my own childhood "suffering," thus allowing me to empathize with Brianna. But on those more upbeat days, I also have to admire the determination my offspring is exhibiting. She absolutely refuses to give up sometimes. The most frequent showcase of this determination is naptimes, but desires to eat ice cream or crackers, to leave the light on all night, or to stay home from accompanying me to the gym also commonly provide arenas for her strength of will. Brianna knows what she wants and she intends to get it, no matter how long it takes or how many times she has to repeat a request/demand. She comes by it naturally, I think.

My mother-in-law sometimes told me I was outspoken. When her observation was made in the middle of a heated discussion, I took this as an insult because most of my husband's family was the opposite of outspoken; I figured they didn't like my way of saying or doing things, that I didn't fit in. But if I indicated that this statement made me feel a little hurt, my sweet little (4-foot-10-and-three-eighths) mother-in-law told me that when I wanted something, I got it — not meaning that I was spoiled, but that I was very determined and I knew how to achieve a goal that was important to me. She admired this quality in me and wished she could be more like that herself. I saw myself through her eyes then and accepted the observation as a compliment. Ever since, I've fondly remembered her saying that (especially now that she has passed on) and always smile at being called "outspoken." Yes, I guess I am.

So as my daughter shows signs of full-blown determination, I am beginning to see myself in her. I might be wrong, but I think every parent wants to see themselves in their children, in some form. Every new mother and father search the faces and bodies of their newborns a few moments after the baby has been born, looking for familiar features. "Oh, look, her nose is a little ski jump just like yours, my sweet" or "Her feet are long, just like my side of the family's." It binds them closer to their child; I think that recognizing physical traits in the baby further convinces the parents that this strange new disruption in their lives wasn't plopped down by an alien stork, but that it is a familiar combination of pieces of themselves.

I did this with each of my children; I watched every day for new signs that they had really come from my body, that my genetic blueprint was stamped clearly on them. (I had to look closely most of the time because at first it seemed that they physically took after my husband much more than they did me, so much so that strangers in the grocery store would actually ask if they were mine, like I was the babysitter or I adopted them.) So now that I see signs of my own personality emerging in my daughter, I am cheering a little to know that there wasn't a mixup in the hospital nursery and that a few years from now we won't be embroiled in a huge, heartbreaking and very public lawsuit.

I have to admit I am a little proud of her. ... Okay, a lot.

For one, it's a little boost to my ego that my own flesh and blood is taking after me. For another, and more important, reason, I am proud that my daughter is going to be outspoken, as her grandmother called it. She can have the power to achieve whatever she can visualize. And ever since my mother-in-law pointed it out to me, I have seen it in myself and in Brianna as a strength, not a weakness. Right now, for my daughter, the strength exhibits itself in little ways: she knows what she wants, whether it's an ice-cream cone or a later bedtime (or no bedtime at all; she may very well be looking to stay awake continuously). Of course, I don't always let her have what she wants because as the parent I know some of it isn't healthy or good for her. But I'm not trying to break her of her determination, the drive to try to get it. Leaching that strength from her would be just as unhealthy in the long run, and heartbreaking to watch.

My mother often has told me she knew when she raised my siblings and me that we would be independent and determined individuals. She accepted that that would mean more work and some agony for her. She reminds me of that when I complain about my frustration with my daughter's endless requests and refusal to give up. My mom was strong enough to allow her children to be themselves, to reach for their dreams, to struggle to get what they wanted. It's worked for us. I'm trying to let it work for my own daughter, so she can be just as much of a dreamer as I always have been, and to know that with persistence and drive, those dreams can become reality.

I have been complaining to anyone who asks about how amazingly frustrating Brianna has been of late. She has tested me on everything, pushed every button I have as a parent and as a person, and then has created more buttons to push on top of the existing ones. She has refused to sleep, she has acted up when we've been out shopping, she has dug in her heels on even the simplest of issues. I have been pulling out my hair on it so much I bet I'll be bald if it keeps up for another week or two. I've tried to stay calm and tried to just stand my ground. I haven't given in, because I know that won't help matters either. I hoped it was merely one of those phases and that if I just stuck it out, Brianna would move past it and I could feel sane again.

What I knew to be true deep-down, however, was that I was part of the source of the problem, or at least most of the solution. Life has been very busy for a few weeks; our calendar has been unusually packed full with activities and events, and we've had more people in our house than usual. I've been all things to all people for a few weeks or more — well, all people but two or three, most noticeably Brianna.

When you're busy, and you're doing seemingly everything for everyone, something's gotta give. That something could be sleep, nutrition, exercise, work, church or community obligations, friends or family. I firmly believe that it is impossible to do everything at once and do it well; inevitably something, or someone, loses. For me, what gets lost is going to be sleep or my husband or children. And this past two weeks is not the first time I've seen evidence of my busy schedule pop up in my daughter's behavior. It's happened before. Have I learned my lesson? Apparently not. But I am trying to pay closer attention now.

I am not saying that I regret my activities or commitments during this time. I wouldn't go back and change what I was doing. Some friends and acquaintances were in real need of my help and I was willing and able to be of assistance. It was a little tiring and taxing at times, but I felt good that I was able to help and give back to others, when I feel that others have helped me so much at times in the past.

But I was short-changing my own daughter's needs and she began letting me know it. She could tell that I was stressed and drained, and she felt nervous that I wasn't on an even keel. That alone is enough to make a small child a little scared or uncertain; they need and expect stability and routine. What's more, my state of mind began affecting how I treated her, and she didn't appreciate the change. She felt sad and scared for me and then angry that she wasn't getting the attention she deserved, so she relayed the message to me loud and clear.

It's taken me a couple of weeks to hear her, even as loud as her messages have been. She doesn't know exactly what she's feeling or what to tell me in words, but with her obnoxious three-year-old behavior Brianna's been saying, "Please love me. Please listen to me. Please pay attention to me. *I* need you, and you're busy with other stuff." I heard what she was saying right away but didn't translate it accurately until recently. I made an effort to be there for her and to parent her properly as all this has been going on, but I didn't put my heart into it. Today, I decided it was time to do it right.

My mother and I have talked about this idea before when life has taken Brianna and me through this same busy-stress cycle, and yesterday I talked to another more experienced, wiser mother than I. The same message came across: all Brianna needs is to feel that I love her and that she has my time and my undivided attention when we are together. That doesn't mean that I quit all of my other obligations completely, but it does mean the rest of the time when life is "normal" she gets the usual, expected, needed amount of time from me and that when we go through the busy cycles, she gets my complete attention when I am not physically involved with other commitments.

It means that I listen to her, really listen, when she tells me something, even if it's just to point out the harmless, tiny bug that's meandering across the floor. It means that I don't read to her or do anything on her clock on autopilot. It means that I hug her and enjoy it, reveling in that embrace as much as she is, instead of responding like a robot, checking off in my mind the next task I am about to do. It means I whisper sweet words of encouragement and sincere praise when I notice she deserves it and needs it. It means I treat her as a human being and not a plant; and not just any human being but my own blood, who I carried around and nourished from my own body for a year and a half of pregnancy and nursing. It means I tap into my heart, my soul, in my everyday relationship with her.

And I notice as soon as I recognize what I'm doing, brushing her off repeatedly because I'm busy thinking about what has to be done or because I just need ever-increasing personal time, I correct in mid-stride and begin loving her again. I observe that the second my attitude toward her changes, her behavior and attitude spin right around 180 degrees. She's the happy, sweet, endearing little creature she's always been.

It's really that simple. It doesn't require more time on my part (she already spends almost all of her time with me) but just a different attitude. Focusing and loving, being in the moment for Brianna does require a little extra energy than I feel I have to give when things are hectic, but it's ten times less than the energy I've been expending trying to get her to just stop being so annoying. When she feels loved and emotionally nourished, she doesn't "act out," as they say, so I don't have to take the time and energy to discipline her. I can still have my spurts of busy-ness, but she doesn't feel deprived of me. And that makes for two much happier people.

CHAPTER 6
I NEED TO GET OUT

Sometimes I feel trapped at home, like a caged animal. I'm a prisoner in a thirteen-hundred-square-foot space, stuck with two crazy inmates who harass me and yell gibberish at me, expecting me to understand and interpret correctly. I'm responsible for the feeding and toileting habits of these inmates as well as their emotional and social well-being. It's as if one of the patients in a mental ward were entrusted with the therapy and healing of her fellow patients. I often don't feel quite up to the task, just ready to abandon my mind to the darkness of lunacy. I long for either solitary confinement or a last-minute grant of clemency to set me free and absolve me of whatever act of defiance that landed me in the cage in the first place.

However, I am a prisoner who possesses her own key out, at least from the physical confines of the space. The key doesn't allow me to walk away permanently from my cage, but it does allow me day trips. And it doesn't do much for the company — the fellow lunatics are attached to me by invisible chains, to hound me wherever I roam. Even knowing that day trips have the potential to make me even crazier, the change of pace from lunacy inside the bin to outside it is tempting.

So I spring myself and my hangers-on for trips — trips to the local store for more diapers, fruit snacks and milk; trips to the big mall an hour away to get pants and shoes that fit; even trips to see Grandma, six hours away. For these jaunts, I always prepare myself with all the necessary supplies as well as with a dollop of extra fortitude. The supplies in the diaper bags — milk, snacks, books and toys — often run out at about the same time as my fortitude, but I still continue to go out because I just *have* to leave my cell — and because, as they say, insanity is defined as continuing to do the same thing over and over and hoping for a different result. I continue to do the same thing and continue to hope for a change in my situation.

We must make quite a sight, my young inmates and I. Harried mom with hair hastily pulled up in a big clip pushes an unwieldy double stroller full of two children and associated stuff. The children may already be fussing as they are pushed toward the door of the mall entrance because they're already tired of sitting after an hour of being straitjacketed into car seats. Now they're strapped for an undetermined amount of time into a new, unyielding harness. The mom approaches the door, assessing the feasibility of getting on the other side of that heavy glass door with only two hands at her disposal. She opens the door with one hand, props it open with her rather squishy rear end, bends gingerly with rear end still propping door, and grabs for the front of the big stroller. She pulls it through the door, all the while trying to keep that bottom in one place, swiveling carefully to get the whole length of said unwieldy stroller through the heavy door. A couple of near-misses ensue in which stroller gets stuck in door as it closes, rear end having slipped elsewhere.

And *then* the shopping can begin.

A whole mall awaits — the favorite department stores and smaller specialty shops, the Taco Bells and Chick-fil-A's, the cookie kiosk exuding the enticing aroma of freshly-baked

chocolate-chip calorie conveyors not too far from the cinna-
mon-roll vendor throwing off its own competing scent of
morning-fresh, cream cheese-frosted diet busters. Somewhere
out there in this obstacle course of shopping exists the perfect
pair of unstained and flattering pants, comfortable yet attractive shoes (not yet scuffed up), and a simple yet sexy enough
top to get Daddy's eyes popping out for just a moment. A
mom can dream.

But to get to those simple pieces of apparel, I must anticipate every fuss, be prepared to stanch any complaints and
pleas to get out. I must be steely. I must be focused on my
goal. I must be flexible, resilient yet firm. It's a tall order, much
like that super-sized diet lemonade I virtuously allow myself at
Chick-fil-A.

Usually, I can explore the first department store without
too much interruption, if I keep it quick and I don't stop anywhere for more than a couple of minutes. The stroller wends
its way through numerous narrow alleys between crammed
clothes hangers, far around the fine-china section of the home
department, in and out of elevators that have been thought-
fully and logically placed so that it is impossible to find them.
The escalator is absolutely not an option. With a single
stroller, a parent can ignore the rule about not using it on the
escalator (or just pop that one kid out for the minute it takes
to get down), but a double stroller, with two kid occupants, is
just out of the question. I search out the elusive salesperson
who might be able to direct me toward the elevator located in
no-man's-land, far off on the periphery of the store. At least
the girls seem to enjoy the elevator rides. The only other drawback is that they then fight over who's going to push the button. Arrrggggh!

I get through that first big store without seeing anything

remotely interesting. Not surprising, since I can only do reconnaissance from a distance of five feet or so from all the racks. I have to go on color and general style. Nice color, but that's the section that's only size twenty. Not for me. Hip style but that size two definitely won't work either. We head out into the mall proper in search of the next shop that is likely to have things to appeal to me, someone who is definitely out of the *Vogue* game (not like I was ever *in* it).

By now, I've already fielded three appeals for fruit snacks. The first two are denied. "Mom–meee, I'm hungry!!" "Mommy, I'm bored!" "Mommy, I want to get out!" The third time, fruit snacks are duly handed over. I am not ready to chase Brianna around quite yet. That will invariably come later. My younger daughter has fussed without words but uncategorically demanded her bottle of milk. I sigh heavily and audibly, the weight of the world pressing the air from my lungs, and pull the first bottle out of the depths of the diaper bag. The two girls are satiated — for about five minutes. I've got a narrow window in which to search my favorite store.

When I find one or two items I actually want to try on, life gets tricky. That definitely means stopping for an undesirable amount of time in one static place, a tiny place to boot. The only salvation possible is that the girls get interested in their reflections in the mirrors. Unfortunately, however, this rarely works because by this time they're past the point of distraction. They're rebelling; the crew is gearing up for mutiny. After changing into clothes that invariably don't look good on me, another hope shot down, I leave the tiny mirrored room with hair dangling in straggly pieces from my clip and hope (dwindling, however) to find something more promising.

By this time I've arrived at another large department store and my children's patience is gone. Marissa has now finished off the bag of crackers and is on her second bottle of milk, close to draining it dry, and I'm out of options with her. She sits and fusses, throwing the empty bottle to the ground. I bend and retrieve it from somewhere in between the wheels of the behemoth stroller. Brianna is bigger and more forceful and her pleas to be set free finally convince me to spring her from her harness. She leaps out and darts off into the underbrush of a full rack of clearance dresses.

"Hey, get out of there! Brianna, no more fruit snacks for you! You're going to be in time out!" Who am I kidding? I have no real recourse. Either I deal with this or I just pack up and go home, which defeats the whole purpose of my driving seventy-five miles to get here in the first place. I wander around the nearby racks, keeping one eye on that one rack that contains my firstborn, the other eye on discounted clothing that might make me look and feel a little prettier, despite the damage that bearing my two little angels has done to my belly and too many other body parts.

She dashes out and runs around a few more racks and then up and down the big aisle a little bit. "Brianna! NOW! Get back here!" My voice hits a warning pitch and I start getting really frustrated. There's just no winning.

It's at this point that I feel I'm really nuts. I wonder why I chose to subject myself to this kind of torture, which I actually had to pay for in the form of gasoline, and I start imagining handing my children over to that maternal stranger of my fantasies who is not in danger of losing her marbles any second. I know that shopping like this is a futile operation, and I rarely accomplish much buying (perhaps a good thing), but in a way I feel a small inkling of satisfaction for knowing I tried — I'm a real stubborn (and masochistic?) gal.

So I feel like the mother from hell sometime during the

middle of the trip, depending both on how low my expectations were at the beginning and how much patience was available for withdrawal in my maternal bank. But much like I have found in my travails at home, there can be rewards later just as sweet and heavenly as were the penalties and hellishness. And there can even be some sweet moments in the midst of the travails, believe it or not, if I focus a little and let them penetrate my hardened, bitter outer shell.

One thing Brianna does that's very cute but hard to really appreciate, at least initially, in my state of near-insanity could be called the "amazing polar thaw."

It works like this: she approaches an icy-cold, tough-looking stranger and makes conversation. Her opening line tends to be, "What's your name?" I've heard it millions of times, it seems. And it's not just something she asks of me or of close friends or relatives. She's asking everyone she comes in contact with. *Everyone.*

So the mall is a great place for her to practice her thawing technique. She's bored, her potential targets are bored, and there are plenty of people to choose from. For example, we're in one big, upscale department store, walking around — I, looking at very pretty clothes far out of my budget if not on clearance (those green or red signs touting sales of 75 percent off make my eyes light up with possibility), and she, investigating wire racks, potted plants and mannequins — when she spots an interesting specimen: a real, live man.

This particular target is an older gentleman, probably retired and forced to sit in malls while his wife takes her sweet time spending his retirement money. Legs wearily spread wide and feet askew on the walkway (he is really quite lucky the store provided nice benches for compelled companions), this dour-looking man stares into space, obvious signals of "leave me alone" radiating out from his haggard visage. To me, he is merely another fixture in a large store filled with merchandise and people willing to buy it. No matter how friendly my inclinations, I have years of experience to be able to recognize when some people just don't want to be bothered. To my chagrin, Brianna demonstrates that she has no years of experience in social niceties. As I stand frozen in that moment watching in horror, she casually yet confidently sidles up to the man and chirps, "What's your name?"

At this point, my natural impulse (as always) is to hastily intercede as quickly as my freeze wears off, as if my daughter's slight *faux pas* is a matter of national security, mumble "I'm sorry" to the man, and then drag my little girl off like a sack of rotting potatoes and explain to her, somehow, that some people just don't want to be bothered. We can't always be friendly, can't always talk to just anyone we see. And not everyone is going to respond happily, especially when their expression to start with is so dour and menacing. I really expect this man to ignore Brianna or mumble a brief reply from the side of his puckered mouth as I shuffle her off from the crime scene.

Amazingly enough, the scenario does not play out as I imagined. The man's dour façade lifts like a garage door, revealing a big softie sitting on the concrete slab within. Brianna's falsetto question and pixie smile act as the automatic door opener, and his inner grampa comes out to play. He looks back cheerfully at Brianna, smiles, and tells her his name. He even strikes up a little conversation with her, stretching to the point that I have to tear them apart so I can move on with my futile shopping venture (which probably would only entail more of Brianna burrowing under racks of clothes and chewing the fat with retirees).

With my daughter's innocent and friendly question, I have watched her transform probably hundreds of people from irascible loners to gregarious grampas. The locale is unimportant — post office lines, grocery stores, bookstores, you name it — there are always frowny-faced men and women who are miraculously changed by a friendly child.

So if I allow myself to thaw out in kind for a moment or two, I can regain some of my equanimity by appreciating her cuteness and gregariousness. I feel a little more relaxed, Brianna immediately senses my newly relaxed state, and we establish a good rapport again for long enough for me to look around a few more racks — and then I get myself and my little inmates the heck out of that mall before either my money or my patience is spent.

I don't limit myself to trips to the mall. A few times a year, I dream big and attempt *long distances*. If loading up in the car for one hour and trekking around a larger city to numerous shops qualifies a mom for the loony bin, then packing the children into a space the size of a modest bathroom for six hours or even more could rival it for stupidity, audacity, or lunacy. The only advantage to being in the car for a good part of a day, rather than going in and out of shops all day, is that you don't have to take the kids in and out of seats too often and encounter that childhood law of physics (inertia — an object at rest is more likely to stay at rest and it takes extra energy to move it from being at rest to being in motion, and then back the other way). That extra energy then can stay with the mom or dad, who have to safely pilot a two-ton vehicle through other crazy drivers and road construction and whiny backseat drivers not old enough to have permits.

I've done an inordinate amount of traveling the past three years, considering I have two small children. I have flown with Brianna six times that I can think of, and once with Marissa (three times, if you count being pregnant with her, which is a significant accomplishment in itself — try reaching down to get coloring books and crayons out of a bag under the seat in front of you when a huge pregnant belly is hogging the already minuscule amount of space between rows). I have driven to my mother's countless times with my children in tow and have taken numerous short trips to numerous places. I haven't gone around the world with my children, as did a family in a book I just read, but I feel I've kept up the usual pace of visiting. These trips, modest in scope for a freewheeling, flexible single or couple, are huge ventures when children are added to the equation.

Our first such venture was the obligatory five-hour drive to my mother's house so friends and family there could meet my six-week-old daughter. She slept almost the entire way there, which was amazing. I was able to sit in the front seat with my husband, quietly enjoying uninterrupted time together, as if our lives had not just been completely rearranged, as if by a tornado, by the arrival of our somewhat chicken-legged but adorable bundle of joy.

On the way home, however, it wasn't as smooth. We sat still or crept for a good hour through road construction near the end of our trip, with our sweet little angel alternately fussing and screaming the whole time, her tiny face diaper-rash red and scrunched up unrecognizably, her thick dark hair matted on her forehead. The challenge was figuring out how to calm her or feed her (note: I was nursing, so I only had a little bit of pumped milk in a bottle) while keeping her safely contained in a car seat. Trying moments (a long sixty minutes' worth of them) like that are the mother of invention: the fiery furnace of learning to be a parent, mainly creating new methods for placating a helpless infant. When we finally cleared the construction and arrived home, where we were able to release our pitiful child from her prison, we breathed huge sighs of relief, and I imagine our blood pressures dropped back to normal, healthy levels.

That fun little experience did not prevent me from making the same trip again, by myself. Just a few months later, I took a huge leap of faith — or insanity — and flew alone cross-country with a five-month-old. She did okay, all things considered, but despite the reassurances of fellow passengers that she was a doll and pretty well-behaved, I still felt guilty for subjecting other travelers to the occasional fussiness of a baby restricted to her mommy's lap for half a day. That's not to mention the toll the trip took on me; I could no longer rest and enjoy the solitude, the time to read, the rush at takeoff, the languid drifting over an expanse of marshmallow clouds.

Every time I flew back and forth to college, I had relished each of those landings and takeoffs, the thrill of the forces against my body, the earth's horizon at an odd tilt, the rapidly shrinking cities with their thousands of inhabitants going about their usual business. I had loved seeing the clouds from above, the long stretch of fluffy cotton rolled out flat with occasional erupting cashmere geysers. When clear of the clouds, I gazed at the flat plains, the grids of fields and country roads, the relief maps of mountains far below me. Window seating was a given. But post-baby, aisle seats were preferable for practical matters: more visits to the tiny closet of a bathroom, more need to get up and roam around to calm a bored infant.

That first flight was the death of my single self; I mourned the loss of those enjoyments.

Again, being my stubborn self, and since I still felt the irresistible urge to travel, to see places and beloved friends and family, I subjected myself and my growing baby to more trips: four more flights, all but one by myself, in the next year or so, and innumerable long drives. My husband and I packed up our child and her numerous accouterments into the car and traveled to southern California and to far northern California, and then to Florida, New York, and of course, Grandma's, once we were back East again. The "trips" page in Brianna's baby book is packed with entries: a chronicle of her introduction to the world and of her mother's penchant for wacky schemes and a short memory.

Regardless of my adult lust for going places, feeling the open road or the open sky, I can still remember vividly how difficult and boring it was to travel as a child. Every summer and Christmas we drove either six or twelve hours (depending on where we lived at the time) to visit my grandparents. My mother would provide each of the three of us children with little bags full of an assortment of foods, such as sandwiches and snacks and even previously frozen fried chicken wings. It was partially to keep us from getting hungry, obviously, but also partially to keep us busy, at least for a short time. Now that we are grown, the joke (unfortunately not an exaggeration) is that my sister in particular would have that entire bag of food devoured shortly after we pulled away from our street, and she would begin asking for more about ten minutes into a twelve-hour trip. So much for keeping her busy.

For my part, I hoped to use sleep as a time-filler. I tried to force myself to fall asleep to while away the dull hours in blissful and quickly-passing unconsciousness, but since it consistently eluded me, I had to keep my mind busy for the full traveling time through the conventional methods of reading, drawing, and arguing with my brother and sister over placement and boundaries in the station wagon. I would even attempt to fall asleep when we passed through tunnels, thinking that at least it would be dark and therefore easier to get to sleep; I never succeeded during the twenty or thirty seconds it took to pass through them.

So I know that it's hard for my children — I've been there. But I continually insist on taking them on trips with me. The reasons could be multitudinous: either I'm a masochist or a sadist, or I'm far beyond optimistic, or I'm extremely stubborn. So on we go to Grandma's or to friends' homes or sightseeing. The results have been reasonable, all things considered. Either I'm just lucky that Brianna is a good little traveler, or she's not old enough to really start bugging me about it from the back seat, or she figures she'd better get used to it because I'm not going to quit. She's been pretty good and I haven't given up yet.

One thing I have learned from all my travels, however, is to plan carefully and to always be prepared. That includes packing as many toys, books, and food items as possible to keep her busy. It also includes planning to stop and to take as much reasonable time as necessary to get ready to return to the road. Gone are the days (unless we just luck out on a short trip to my mom's) that I can hop in my car and drive, pushing myself Spartan-like toward my destination, with either no stops or a thirty-second bathroom break.

As children-toting travelers, gone are those days of freedom — we must expect to take a good, thorough break and not push our girls to move on until they are ready to do so. The one or more breaks include diaper changes and lunch and drinks and a little bit of run-around, stretch-out-the-legs time.

So we know to be prepared and to stop at regular intervals. If I'm driving to my mom's, which I've done many times now, the regular intervals often fall at the same stops on every trip. But the next, most important lesson comes here: flexibility is crucial. Sometimes you just have to stop an extra time, even if it's only thirty minutes — or thirty seconds! — after the regular stop. This can be difficult, because as easy as it is to get accustomed to making regular stops with children, it is a little more of a challenge to get the hang of just stopping when your adult common sense sees there is no reason for it. But that flexibility factor makes all the difference in the world.

I've found that being flexible also has enriched my journey through life, just like it eases the pain of my jaunts to my mom's house; those unexpected stops that frustrated me at first have made the rest of the trip more pleasant, more purposeful, more worthwhile. The stops weren't just refueling to allow me to continue my trip; they became part of the trip, the whole package a grand and glorious adventure.

So regardless of the hassles involved — the extra time, equipment, and patience required to travel with one small child and even two — I have persevered in my wanderings. I relish the actual journey by air or by car, and I always love to see my family and friends. But another key component in my traveling is an undeniable, visceral thirst for adventure. On one of my more recent trips to my mother's (believe me, those six-hour drives alone have significantly contributed to filling up those baby book pages), I realized that the glorious freedom to do what I want and enjoy, even if it's fettered a bit by my children, was a driving force in my persistence.

Knowing I could stop (and had to) whenever I wanted and to share these jaunts with my little girls was liberating and thrilling. I also realized it was a great gift to be able to spend such unlimited time with my darling offspring and to instill in them the same wanderlust and *joie de vivre*. Not least of all, their very presence and personalities and reactions to our little activities spurred me on and reminded me that this is what life is all about; this is why I had children: to share, to teach, to just have fun together.

On this trip to Grandma's, I was in no hurry. Mom wouldn't be home when we arrived anyway and wouldn't be until late at night, so I figured I might as well make all the stops my children required of me. I took my time with everything; we parked at a Cracker Barrel along the way and went inside for a solid hour and a half. I made sure we all went potty and had diapers changed when we first arrived and when we were ready to pile back into the car. We took our time in that bathroom. It gave Brianna the freedom to talk to as many other restroom visitors as she wanted to, to peek under the stalls (and be reprimanded for doing so), to wash her hands repeatedly, and to wander around and chat and release pent-up energy.

After our necessary visit to the powder room, we proceeded to the dining area. We sat right next to the checkerboard and the fireplace, by chance, which turned out to be fortuitous. I parked Marissa in a high chair and funneled a continuous stream of bite-size food to her, thus keeping her happy, and sat Brianna in a big people chair on my other side, where she ate just enough not to feel hungry anymore. After that, she wandered over to the checkerboard and played a very long game of solitaire checkers. While Marissa stayed content with her pile of food (a sizeable percentage of which became a pile around the base of the chair), Brianna ran around a bit (still within close range of me) and had a great time playing her game. I'm sure she was happy I wasn't rushing her. When we were all completely finished eating and playing (and I'd even enjoyed a delicious blackberry cobbler, since I was going all-out here), I made the final trip to the bathroom to clean up and settled us all comfortably in the car. The rest of the trip was quiet, uneventful and even enjoyable.

Even though it was not the kind of trip I used to make pre-children, unfettered and free and alone, I had adjusted finally to the reality of my new traveling style and had figured out how to optimize the chances for a good, smooth trip. The girls actually had a hoot, despite being cooped up in a car for six hours, and I enjoyed the time with them. It was our own "Mom and Girls' Big Adventure," out in the big world, the freeway at our feet, the attractions of a simple country restaurant and even rest stops practical enough yet exotic and new enough to keep us entertained. Mom and the girls were a team, a dauntless crew of "game" hunters enjoying the car safari.

Even on the days when I'm not taking my girls and all our equipment on another visit to Grandma's, I'm reminded that life itself is an adventure, each new day offering up about nine hundred waking minutes of endless possibilities. Brianna's demeanor every morning doesn't let me forget that she expects only the best out of her day. She strides into my room confidently and cheerfully almost every day, padding across the hallway and hopping into bed with me, saying "good morning!" in a chipper voice or flashing a winning, open smile. She snuggles down under the covers next to me and says "I love you" and just cuddles or decides that it's time to play. The latest game is simply titled "Find me!" She throws the covers over her head and prompts me with "Where's Brianna?" I am expected to ask this repeatedly, all the while running my hands along the top of the covers, feeling the lump created by her small body, throwing out possibilities of what actually lies underneath my quilt. After some wrong guesses ("A rock? A snake? A turtle?"), I finally am graced with the appearance of Brianna, either playing herself or a cute little puppy or a scary lion. The day proceeds from there.

My choice from that point in the morning is to play along with Brianna, treating the day as an adventure, even if our routine stays pretty much the same as the days before, or to take that routine and adhere to it cheerlessly, morphing into a jaded drill sergeant with no desire for enjoying the time I've been blessed with, making everything I do a chore. I have to feed and clean up after the girls and do laundry and put them down for naps and all the usual things, but what matters is the spirit in which I do it. The choice I try to make when faced with my day and all its necessities is to enjoy the time I have with my girls, being adventurers even in familiar territory. It makes all the difference in the moods and outlooks of both my girls and me. I don't travel a freeway every day, but I do travel life's highway, and I hope I can remember to enjoy the ride, just as Brianna does naturally.

PART III
FULL HEART – MOMENTS

CHAPTER 7
LIVE IN THE MOMENT

I got honked at today because I stopped at a yellow light. As I looked in my rearview mirror, the driver behind me was waving his arms in my direction, indicating furiously that I was a complete idiot for stopping before a turning light had been red for a few seconds. I admit that I breeze right through many a yellow light (some closer to red than others), but this time I was a visitor in my mom's state and I was feeling cautious or more law-abiding than usual. Since I was just headed to the gym for a workout, I wasn't in a hurry, or I might have blown caution to the wind as I do at other times. But the guy behind me must have had a real need to be somewhere important and fast, since he got so angry at my whim of obeying the law.

Or maybe he didn't have to be anywhere — this time. Maybe he was in such a habit of having to be somewhere *now* that when he ended up behind me he plum forgot that his honking was unnecessary. Maybe just the night before he had been trying to get his extremely pregnant, in-transition-labor wife to the hospital before she crowned and gave birth, and he was so sleep-deprived that he forgot that twelve hours had passed and his brand-new son had been born already and was crying ceaselessly in the hospital's nursery. Who knows? But what I do know is that, whether he had to be at an important business meeting a block away in thirty seconds or whether he was just heading out to the golf course for some relaxation, he felt a real need to get angry at me for complying with traffic signals. And that a fleeting fifteen seconds later, both of us went through the light when it turned green again.

I can't say that I've never been in this man's shoes. I've gotten a little annoyed with other drivers who don't seem to appreciate just how vital it is that I shave ten seconds off my driving time at every possible juncture so I won't be a minute later for an appointment of some kind — community and church duties, doctor's visits, even sometimes personal time. How could they not know that I simply *must* get there early, or the world will come to a screeching halt? How dare they slow me down? They just don't get it. Such inconsiderate people in today's society!

I cannot count the number of times (in one day, no less) that I have told my daughter, "Hurry up! We've got to hurry!" She'll be miles behind me as I'm trying to get us all into the car to pick up groceries or get to the pediatrician's office; then she'll lag behind as I attempt to get us all out of our respective car seats, and then as I try to dash down the sidewalk and into a building. As I'm trying to rush her along and shave any possible seconds off our journey to our destination, she's stopping at every possible opportunity: to gaze at flowers, bushes, ants, other people, cars, a pair of Barney shoes five miles away. Even when we went as a family to Disney World, we as parents were excited to get to our next ride or show, and Brianna was always behind us, stopping to watch other kids or to look at the bricks in the walkway. I would have thought she'd be just as interested as we were in getting to the next ride, but she surprised me there. I didn't generally find it amusing, either, particularly for the price I had to pay to see those shows. For her to watch other kids or ants on the walk, we could have stayed home and enjoyed those activities for free.

No matter what the activity, the difference between us is the same: I'm focused on the task at hand, which is getting to my destination. I'm focused on the result, the end, something that isn't happening right now. Brianna is focused on the present second: whatever looks interesting right there, right now, in front of her face. Since our two goals clash, allowing the achievement of only one — and since I'm the adult and get to make the decisions drawing on the wisdom of my years — I rush her along, trying to distract her from the things she is examining, and trying to convince her that getting somewhere really is much more interesting and important than the fascinating scenes along the way.

It's practically an impossible task, and a very frustrating one from my viewpoint. I like to get things done; I don't want to have to stop and answer Sphinx's riddles on my way to my destination. Maybe it's so difficult to get my little charge to cooperate because our destinations really aren't any more interesting than what we see along the way. (Disney may be an exception, but since she didn't see it that way, maybe even the manmade glories there were no comparison with what existed naturally.) The doctor's office is hardly a picnic. No wonder I can't get her to hurry up so she can "enjoy" all the things we have to get done.

Even with some of the things we're doing that *are* fun, such as going to see animals in a zoo or playing with a friend who has great toys, it's still a weighty challenge to get her to hurry along so we can do them. But when I think about it, what is the point of hurrying through one or five things you are doing that are very interesting just to get to do something else that is equally interesting? If you're eating a chocolate ice cream cone, are you going to hurry through because you're being told that you get a strawberry one next, and a vanilla one after that? Might as well enjoy the chocolate one while you've got it.

So it all boils down to a simple concept that is certainly not new to me or my daughter: enjoy the ride, live in that moment. Because most of people's lives nowadays seem to be spent in transit to one destination after another, if all we do is focus on where we're going next, we'll spend our lives ignoring the trip, the ride, the present moment. And since we spend so much time on the way to somewhere, that's logically where most everything happens, not wherever it is we're going.

Since I'm being forced to face this trait in myself, thanks to my short guru, I try now to ask myself several things when I catch myself hurrying (I also admit I'm lucky because I have a built-in alert system, my three-year-old, that automatically blares at me when I'm hurrying). First, am I really in a hurry? Does my life depend on getting to my destination five seconds earlier? Much of the time I have absolutely no time constraints at all; I'm just accustomed to the idea of hurrying. Second, if I really am in a crunch to get somewhere important, I ask myself, What can I do next time to give myself a bigger lead time so I don't have to stress myself like this? I've gotten better at trying to be better prepared, especially when I have a child or two in tow. Last, I ask myself, If there really is no dire need to arrive somewhere fast, what can I enjoy along the way so the journey can be more pleasurable? There's always something, like the changing colors of fall leaves or wispy white clouds drifting in a cornflower-blue sky. Sometimes it's silly, strange details like a sign hanging upside down or a new color of paint on a house I frequently pass on a well-traveled route.

My daughter is enjoying the ride. It should be so easy for me to join her. I think we'll slow down and look at some ladybugs together.

Back when Brianna was either just a twinkle in my eye, as they say, or a newly arrived infant, I had read somewhere in my ton of literature that in disciplining young children, it was important to give them a consequence of negative behavior either immediately or very soon after the behavior occurred so they would be able to make the connection between the two and remember the next time that the consequence was linked to the behavior (therefore, we hope, deterring them from committing that negative act again). If the parent put off a "time out" until a few hours later, the very young child might not make that connection, and then the whole disciplinary endeavor would be utterly wasted.

I do believe Brianna is getting past the stage where discipline has to be split-second immediate, but she isn't to a stage where I could tell her she can't play with her Little People farm this weekend because she grabbed one of the farm animals from her baby sister. I'm not sure if she has the concept of "tomorrow" yet, or even "later" or anything other than a window of a few hours. Today is the only day that is real for my three-year-old, a charming trait that is at once galling and instructive.

For me, on the other hand, "today" is often not real or at least not very important; it's just some stopover on my way to tomorrow. I often tell myself to hang in there, to "get through" today so I can arrive at tomorrow, and then find that tomorrow is just the same as today — but not learning my lesson, once again I try to get through it too, on my way to some magically and radically different future.

I've been a longtime offender of living for the future. Since my early teen years, I can remember working hard so I could have a better ... whatever. I worked hard in high school, religiously cracking books and staying heavily and ridiculously involved in extracurricular activities that would plump up my scholarship application. I couldn't wait to get out of high school and get to college. I knew exactly where I wanted to go and how to get there. I did it, but I wonder if maybe I could have figured out how to relax a little and enjoy each day while I was on my way to college.

In college, as much as I enjoyed my social life and many of the classes I took, I still found myself waiting some days for a better day to come along: during the week I looked forward to the weekend, particularly if I had a very exciting date planned. I waded through the morning's classes so I could take a nap or talk with friends in the afternoons. If it was freezing cold on my morning walk to class across campus, I eagerly anticipated warmer weather; of course, when warmer weather came, it was so hot outside that the buildings were artificially cooled as cold as it had been on some of my morning walks.

After two or three years of college, I began to eagerly anticipate graduation, getting a job and entering the "real world." I grew tired of the student life and was interested in working and earning money in my chosen career. When I began working, however, I found that I missed the plentiful free time and relative freedom of college life and wished I could go back.

I looked forward to getting married and was very excited when I found a kind, caring, fun, dedicated man for a husband. After a few years and a couple of children, I find I sometimes miss the freedom of single life and the ability to do what

I want when I want to do it, like taking trips or shopping alone, without two children to haul in and out of a car at five different stops.

Now I can't wait till my children are old enough to be in school, till we have student loans from my husband's graduate degree paid off, till we can get a bigger house or a second car, till I publish my book, till I lose five or ten more pounds, till I can go to Europe or Mexico. The list goes on and on. I think constantly about this book. I feel that maybe I'll be completely satisfied when I've finished it and it hits bookstores. But I know that as excited as I will be and as happy as I will be that I have accomplished a longtime goal, it won't change my outlook. I'll probably start thinking about publishing the next book. Frankly, in my lucid moments, I find this putting-off-life-for-later way of life pretty pitiful.

Then there's Brianna. She has no big plans for tomorrow. All she wants is to be able to do the things she likes today. She wants to play with her toys, watch videos, see friends and family, read with Mommy, and, most recently, go roller-skating (we read about it in a book and she's fixated on it). If she enjoys a particular activity, she does it now, and revels in it, focuses on it and doesn't think past it.

I spoil even the happy moments or small victories by too quickly thinking ahead to the next happy moment. But I have been catching myself more lately and trying to change my *modus operandi*. This is largely thanks to Brianna, in part because she's a good example of *carpe diem*, and in part because she deserves to be the recipient of my focused, undivided attention, at least sometimes.

One example is our reading time. We spend a good half hour, on average, reading together at naptime and bedtime every day. That's a solid hour every day of one-on-one time, enjoying an activity that has always been one of my favorite pastimes. In that hour, not only is Brianna learning how to read and developing her own skills for storytelling and imagining, but she is learning that I care enough about her to spend "quality" *and* "quantity" time with her. My time with her teaches her that I love her and that she is a special individual, worthy of my best efforts.

I am embarrassed to say that some afternoons and evenings I am marking time, *dying* to get out of her room so I can do something else, like sleep, eat ice cream, play on the computer, spend time with my husband, or even read a more complicated book than Spot. I am human, after all. I am not saying that any of these activities are not worthwhile or necessary for my own learning, sanity, peace of mind, happiness, whatever, but that I am spending twice the amount of time on them by thinking about them and then doing them. And I am short-changing my daughter by thinking about my own activities on her clock. I am going to spend that half hour reading with her no matter what I do next; being impatient and focusing on my next activity won't make the time pass faster, and it won't make my own time alone any more enjoyable. What it will accomplish, however, is making me frustrated and annoyed with Brianna, and she won't get as much out of our time together as she could and should.

So during reading time, I'm consciously trying to put out of my mind my planned activities and working hard on focusing on the very moment I am living. It sounds crazy, but it is sometimes very difficult work to live in the moment because I am so firmly entrenched in the habit of jumping forward in my head while absent-mindedly going through the motions of the present. I find that when I am successful in focusing on the moment, I feel curiously light and free and at peace. Only one train is slowly lumbering along the tracks of my mind, instead of five or ten whizzing by at lightning-speed and changing tracks left and right.

On that one train, I clearly hear Brianna's enchanting voice asking me questions in her clear and complex speech, adding her own background information about the story and the characters drawn on the page, and matter-of-factly pointing out letters and numbers. I thrill to the idea that she has learned to identify all the letters of the alphabet and that she can count to ten and higher and can read the numbers. I realize that the time we have spent together has helped her learn. I recognize how much she has grown in a short period of time and how fast time flies. I realize that by tomorrow, she will have learned something new. At those times, I reluctantly leave her room when we are finished with the requisite number of books, and I feel satisfied with the time we have spent and not eager to move on to my next task or even to time alone.

Living in the moment makes me amazingly more sane and patient. It has helped remind me that no matter how much I mull over a situation and imagine I have things planned in such a way that I will be prepared for all possible scenarios, it is still in the future and the outcome will not be determined until the moment arrives. I cannot will something to happen simply by thinking about it ten thousand times as I try to get to sleep or as I try to read to my daughter. It's going to play out the way it darn well wants to. When I found myself in a dentist's office for almost an hour and a half this morning, I didn't fret about the time it was subtracting from my only day alone of the week; I simply sat quietly. First, while I waited in the lobby for the opportunity to have my teeth cleaned, I finished a book I was reading. Then, as I lay back completely prone in the chair, my mouth full of grit from the polishing tool, waiting for the dentist to check over the work the hygien-ist had performed, I closed my eyes and breathed deeply in and out, savoring the quiet and the time alone with my thoughts. I found I was able to stay in the present without making the leap to hyperspace, and consequently I found myself less angry, less frustrated and impatient. I was at peace. I was accepting of the moment that had been surprisingly sprung on me.

One of my favorite savored moments in time is that of hugging my daughter. We run so many errands that I put her in and out of her car seat countless times a week. I sometimes pluck her out of her seat and set her down on the ground while I run around to the other side of the car to repeat the process with her baby sister. But on other times, I pick her up and hold her as I walk to the other side of the car. On a few occasions now, she has put her arms around my neck, wrapped her legs around my waist and hugged. I have found myself in those moments hugging back with all my might, in no hurry for the hug to end. It is such a precious gift to have my own flesh and blood, packaged in such an irresistibly cute little body, show me that she loves me and appreciates my love for her. I have stood for several minutes in various parking lots just enjoying the hug for as long as possible. I have to pat myself on the back that I haven't cut it short and told my daughter that I only have enough time in my schedule for a fifteen-second embrace, and let's get on to the grocery store now. I must be growing.

CHAPTER 8
SAVOR THE SWEET

Sitting here at my computer, I am finishing up a leftover-from-Easter Cadbury Cream Egg, trying not to get the gooey chocolate that has melted from the warmth of my hands onto the keyboard. I just adore my cream eggs, much like my mom does, and am very sad when the last bite is gone. I could eat them like my husband does, in almost one giant, less-than-five-second gulp, but I choose to take my time with them. I slowly unwrap the colorful, crackly foil, take a small nibble off one end of the egg, and allow the first smooth, creamy, decadent wave of chocolate heaven to wash over me. At this stage, I have only eaten probably one-tenth of the egg. After a moment has passed, and I have eked out the most pleasure I will get out of that small sampling, I proceed with the bacchanalia. I take slow, careful, completely-savored bites, enjoying fully each taste of brown velvet. I wallow in that flavorful mud as long as possible. I can probably stretch out a single egg for a good two to three minutes, taking five to six bites, at the minimum. I make those 180 calories count, by golly! If I'm going to indulge, I'm going to enjoy it for as long as possible and get the most out of it as possible.

My daughter tends to do the same thing. I'm not sure if it's for the same reasons or not; obviously she's not calorie-conscious. She's never heard of a calorie. She's small for her age, rather thin and extremely cute; my bet is she'll be thin all her life and able to eat whatever she wants without gaining a pound, just like her dad. So she can eat as much as she wants, and at this age, she needs to eat so she can grow. But she is aware that quantities are limited, just for different reasons than they are for me. She knows I'm only going to give her one of whatever she's getting, be it a cookie, piece of candy, or ice cream scoop. So she, too, probably figures she has to make it last. She can stretch out her sweet experience for even longer than I can. She takes small bites, savors them, and focuses just on the bite while she is taking it.

Savoring every bite of my calorie-rich candy is something I've been trying to extend to the (potentially) meaning-rich moments of my time. It's a skill I've always had but that I've had to revive being a mom. For one thing, it is crucial to a mom's sanity to be able to enjoy the nuggets of sweetness amongst the rubble of frustration, short temper and sour diapers. So I've had to resurrect this ability so I can stay sane and mostly pleasant day to day. And while my daughter has been a big contributor to my lack of sanity and patience, she has also been a great reminder of just how to implement this ability to savor the moment. She's done it naturally and sweetly by her actions and words and even her very being.

Brianna doesn't slow down much. She's constantly on the go, running from living room to kitchen to bedroom and back, pausing momentarily here and there to eat or to draw. Even as I look at photographs of her, which deceptively seem to depict her sitting still as an ancient statue, I can see by the look in her eyes and some kind of tenseness in her muscles that she is in reality ready to spring to her next activity. Inducing her to sleep, which obviously involves her lying motionless for an hour or two, takes a good half-hour of calming tactics like reading and singing that lull her to a quieter, stiller state. This whole process — watching her run around and getting her to stop — drains my energy. People used to tell me they envied *my* energy level, but I'm thinking now that Brianna sapped that from me in utero. Like a tiny alien from a sci-fi movie, she sucked the life force out of me, and I'm merely a dried-up mother shell.

So most of the time, Brianna isn't known for sporting a calm, relaxing temperament; there's simply too much energy bursting out of her cells to allow her to radiate calm. But I have noticed that on some occasions she can be as soothing as a babbling brook running through a soft green pasture and as gentle as a duckling's downy young feather.

As part of our calm-down ritual, we read and sing lullabies. Sometimes we sit for a minute or two on the small rocking chair adjacent to her bed. After the reading and singing are over, I tuck Brianna in and she requests her animals to be placed next to her on the bed (often two by two, precisely as she directs) and for her two special blankets to be spread out just so near her feet (it's summertime right now so it is much too hot to lay them on top of her body, which is really her first choice).

The last step in the bedtime ritual is the hug and kiss. Every day and evening must include the foundation mutual hug and kiss, but then the pattern varies day to day. Often, Brianna and I share a "big squeeze," during which I lean down to her as she lies prone on her bed and hug her as tightly as I can considering my mechanical disadvantage; at the same time, she wraps her little arms as far around my back as she can reach and squeezes hard. Sometimes we then move on to a "little hug," which means I barely put my hands down behind her back, and she limply rests her hands on my shoulders. We stay a little distance apart and don't throw ourselves into this embrace. What I find amusing is the facial expressions that accompany her end of the deal. With a "big squeeze," she grimaces (in a happy way) and contorts her face, showing that she is indeed putting all her energies into this tight hold. With a "little hug," she half-closes her eyes as if a camera caught her off-guard and relaxes her facial muscles along with the rest of her body. Her whole being participates in our hugs.

Sometimes after we finish our hugs, I walk to the door, and just as I reach it, I get a callback, and the hug procedure repeats itself. And sometimes, on occasions I wish were part of every night's rituals, Brianna pauses after a hug, while our faces are still close together, and brings her hand to my cheek with a delicacy I wouldn't suspect she had if I recalled only her daytime energies. She strokes my face softly, gently, completely lovingly, and gazes at me with eyes that speak wellsprings of tenderness. She clearly and warmly whispers to me, "I love you so much, Mom." For that moment, I feel as if we have switched roles, and I am the young daughter in need of reassurance that I am loved, and she is the all-wise, thoroughly loving mother who is able to provide me that reassurance with one soft caress and a short but potent and sincere phrase. As she looks at me with those eyes that seem to belong to one much more mature and perfect, my heart melts and turns to a warm, thick elixir that coats the entire inside of my body with free-flowing but long-lasting liquid love. I walk away feeling drunk, woozy with love and gratitude that I decided to become a mother, and that I stick with it even during the many days that challenge me to my limit.

Brianna is perceptive. She knows when I'm down and she knows when I've been stretched to or past my uttermost capacities for patience and giving. Sometimes she uses that perception to her advantage to test me, to see if I'll give in and allow her treats before dinner or the freedom to avoid a bath or bedtime. But when she knows I am sad about something that has happened, that I have been disappointed or faced rejection, she comes to me and gently strokes my face or sits on my lap and tries to reassure me. She hugs me, touches my arm, in general reminds me that she cares by physically connecting with me. My husband tries to protect me in those moments I am down, kindly urging me to steal some precious alone time to recoup. In so doing, he usually closes a bedroom door and tells Brianna to leave Mommy alone. But, to my surprise, I have found that I don't always need to be alone, and if she creeps inside that closed door to give me that tender touch, I always welcome it and find myself feeling instantly better. I feel cheered, encouraged, reminded that despite my momentary setback or disappointment, the world can't be too bad if there is a little girl as sweet as Brianna inhabiting it, right here in my very own home.

As we settled in for our bedtime reading routine last night, Brianna decided to change the setting slightly. Instead of our usual posture of lying down next to each other and reading with the book above our heads, we sat up. Big detour from the usual custom. She told me to sit at the edge of the bed that butts up against the wall, propping myself with my back on the wall. She sat next to me and snuggled in to my arm a bit. After a few minutes, she grabbed one of her treasured blankets (a precious one sewn and cross-stitched by a close friend) and put it over her legs. Since she has two of those special blankets, she arranged the other one over my legs, explaining, "So you don't get cold." Then she settled back for a moment and apparently realized she could be more cozy if she had a little pillow behind her back. She reached for a pillow and, telling me to lean forward, placed it carefully where the small of my back would rest. After she was satisfied that I was comfy, she found a pillow for herself and then re-settled her blanket. We were both warm and cozy and fully prepared to enjoy our reading time.

I was touched by her thoughtfulness and told her so. How sweet of her to think of my comfort even as she was arranging for her own. Since we were both in this little venture together, she made sure that we were both as happy as possible. Even after I left her room, reading time over, I smiled, feeling loved because of her small act of kindness and her ability to think of someone else's needs along with her own.

Brianna has shown me this before, a willingness to help and the ability to think about what I might need. When I sneeze several times and my nose starts running, she hops up immediately and runs for my bedroom, coming back with a Kleenex. Her proffering of a simple gift, one that perfectly suits my needs at a given time, is better than any planned or contrived substitute, a generic present given simply because the occasion calls for it. She isn't old enough to know something like that exists, and she isn't old enough to have money to buy me a grand treat. She's just old enough to know what she is able to give.

Perhaps she inherited this ability from my husband. He is

a pro at the "little things that matter most." He daily shows me of his love by his desire to be useful and helpful. Last week, for instance, I made Jell-O. I spruced it up a bit by adding bananas and crushed pineapple, a combination my mother used occasionally when I was growing up and which was my favorite (above just peaches or pears or some other simple addition to that boxed salad/dessert). The only drawback with putting bananas in gelatin is that they continue to ripen and grow darker in color as they sit in the refrigerator. If you eat it within a day or two, it's not a big deal. But if allowed to sit longer, you end up with perfectly good gelatin covered with brown, mushy, unappealing old fruit. This was the case with our Jell-O this week; I made it, we ate half, and it sat in the refrigerator untouched for almost a week because we ate out a few times.

My husband, the thoughtful and conscientious man that he is, informed me about three days after I made this Jell-O that he had eaten the bananas off the top before they got mushier. So last night, when we finally got around to eating the remainder, it tasted perfectly good, retained its jelled state, and was still appetizing. If he hadn't eaten those bananas, I probably would have been inclined to leave that orange-and-pineapple concoction alone forever, hoping that the refrigerator elves would take it away so I wouldn't have to deal with it (not that they ever *do* quietly throw out anything old and moldy; I have to do that gross job myself, but I still hope).

It seems silly, but after my husband told me he had eaten those bananas, I felt a little freer and happier. I had a little burden (mushy, gross, brownish-gray bananas) lifted from my shoulders. I could rest for a few days, knowing that I didn't have to hurry to eat that Jell-O. Neither the gelatin nor the pineapples would go bad by the time I got to eat them. I wouldn't have to worry about throwing it out in a few weeks. Last night, we easily finished off that Jell-O, and it was delicious. All thanks to my husband, who consistently and constantly finds ways to make life a little easier for his wife and family. I feel loved because he eats mushy bananas. I know he wouldn't do that for just anyone. I am worth eating brown bananas for!

My parents' genes could have a hand in my daughter's thoughtfulness, too. Both did many little things for me as I grew up and still do now that I'm grown. My mom read to me, taught me to cook, took me places, as is evidenced in the many other things I've written in this very book. One little thing I appreciated a great deal was her cooking breakfast. She didn't usually have breakfast ready and waiting for us in the mornings; most mornings, we children would just trickle into the kitchen and ask her "What's to eat?". She always rattled off the standard list of suggestions: "Eggs, cereal, pancakes, french toast, oatmeal ...". It was nothing new. I guess we just kept asking in the hopes that an exciting new choice would magically appear in the list, but every day it was the same. My brother and sister often had cereal or pancakes, and I resorted to leftovers: cold spaghetti, casseroles, whatever was in the fridge.

But on random Saturdays, I occasionally woke up to the heavenly scent of batter turning into golden-brown, steaming waffles. Many of the houses we lived in were two-story, and even in the ones that were just one floor, my room was far away from the kitchen, so by the time the waffle smell had wafted like a charmed snake back through my bedroom's closed door, they were usually ready for immediate consumption. By the time I woke up completely and dashed down to the kitchen table, a stack of waffles was sitting on a plate just for me. Now whenever I cook waffles for my family and guests, I reflect on those special Saturday mornings. My mom loved me and I knew it because she made me waffles.

My father — aficionado of classical music, media critic and college professor known (for good and ill) for expecting the best out of his students (and his children) — had his own way of showing he cared. I don't recall many big trips to any fancy places. We had two family vacations to Disney World and a fair number of day trips to zoos and amusement parks. I enjoyed those greatly and still have souvenirs and pictures taken with my cheap little camera. But what made a consistent difference in our lives were the daily and weekly visits to local haunts and strolls through the outdoors around our houses. Dad took us on walks along the lanes through the countryside and on small trails in the woods. He frequently took us to little museums wherever we lived; one was a military history museum that featured old cannons and other weapons and dioramas. It also sported a small pond out front that attracted ducks most of the time, so I think we probably went to the museum more often than not just to feed the ducks. As Dad headed out the door with his three small kids, Mom handed him a bag of old bread, and we happily shared it with our little feathered friends.

One place we went, near the stadium at Penn State University, was a nature preserve of some type with an official name, but all I remember calling it was the "deer farm." It was a very large area of woods, with a wire-fence enclosure that kept in deer and other wild animals. For a small child, to walk around the perimeter of this enclosure took a very long time, so we usually stuck to a limited section of fence near the entrance. Dad gathered up the three of us and Mom gave us each a huge handful of dried corn and other stored-food staples to feed to the deer. We would cluster around the fence and stick our hands through the wire at the "deer farm" and the deer would shyly wander up to the fence and lick our palms clean. I was always fascinated by how rough and large their tongues were. We couldn't get enough of that place.

Dad took us swimming when it was warm enough. Rarely was it in a pool. Looking back, I think a regular public pool would have been too dull and boring. Instead of a standard, one-size-fits-all concrete hole in the ground, we frequented unique, natural swimming locales. Several were lakes and ponds; one was a large creek. This creek had trees on either side and a few benches nearby for picnics. It was quiet, secluded, peaceful. The water was fairly deep in the middle but shallow on the edge, so it suited any age. When I got adventurous, I could try to swim through the deeper part over to the other side. The water flowed fairly quickly there in that deep section, so I never did that alone. No matter, my dad was always there for supervision. We made many visits to that creek, just we and our dad. (I'm thinking all these visits with Dad did double duty as precious alone time for my busy mom.) Dad took pictures of many of our outings, so we have documented for all time my sister eating a banana while propped on a big rock; my little brother, till sporting scars from his chicken pox, playing near the water; and me wearing an upside-down bikini (my mother never let my dad live down that he couldn't put it on right-side-up). We had a good time together.

My father took us three kids on group outings and also spent time with us one-on-one on a regular basis. My favorite dates alone with Dad were to musical events. We saw *The Nutcracker* performed by a talented ballet company, listened to various orchestras filling concert halls with the richly layered strains of classical music, watched plays. I grew up with a deep appreciation for the arts, and for butter-rum Life Savers, since we never failed to stop at the grocery store to buy the little rolls of candy to suck on while we enjoyed culture.

My dad took us many places, few of which would garner more than a fleeting sentence (if that) in some guidebook of places to go and things to see. Most of our activities were free of charge. All lodge in my memory as happy destinations because my dad took the time to take us out frequently and consistently, almost as if on a schedule. He showed us he loved us by just spending time with us doing simple, little things, by showing us the world we lived in and giving us his time and attention.

Even today, my sixty-two-year-old father takes thirty-year-old me on daddy-daughter, one-on-one outings. We go to lunch alone together, just to have time to talk. It's a minor investment for the food and a couple of hours out of his day. Nothing big, really, but I've felt most special to him when we're alone, when it's just us talking about the things we both enjoy: books, higher education, films, the media. Even though I'm no longer his little girl, I still need that time to know that I'm important, that he respects my opinions and how I spend my time, how I use my talents.

Those little gifts of time and attention and thoughtful tiny acts of kindness are still the most important to me, whether they come from my daughter, my parents, my husband, or friends. I always am reminded that someone cares about me when they just listen to me talk about a bad day or when, after listening, they send me a little note of encouragement or a little gift that was related to what I was talking about. None cost much money or time.

One of my favorite bits of wisdom from my religion's canon is this "Out of small things proceed that which is great." I like this quote so much because I know it's true — I've seen it in action, from day one with my parents up until the present. My parents gave the small things to me constantly, reminding me they loved me and wanted the best for me. My daughter gives to her mother what she can with her limited tangible resources, by running to the within-reach Kleenex box in my room to help me with a runny nose. My husband, even with a good job and greater financial and practical resources, still makes me happiest by eating gross-looking bananas. It would be difficult for me to deny that I am loved, and that assurance certainly qualifies as "that which is great."

I've given birth to two children now. That pregnancy and birth process didn't exactly do wonders for my body. If I look at my birthday suit in my bedroom full-length mirror, I get an eyeful. It seems I'm looking at a relief map of rough terrain, a landscape that has experienced a mighty earthquake, one that has irreparably and completely altered the face of the land. I see valleys that once existed as mountains and mountains that rise as great lumps in the place of valleys. Innumerable rutted riverbeds of stretch marks, silvery and shiny and empty of water, stream across my gently sloping stomach and legs and other rounded hills. The distended skin of my stomach is loose and baggy, and combined with the sagging muscles underneath, my midsection is like a huge, windswept sand dune. I can't say that the map pre-baby was of a perfect planned community, but now it's a post-battle wasteland. It's not a pretty picture.

When I rise in the morning or get ready for bed at night, I get another eyeful of my reflection in my medicine-cabinet mirror. My hair isn't as thick as it once was, hormones and stress depleting my head of some of its volume. My eyes are often bleary, lack of sleep robbing the whites of their brightness. My face has a few too many bumps and acne marks on it, hormones and lack of sleep both contributing. The skin around my eyes and mouth seems to be showing signs of fine lines, which are honestly results of my smiling frequently at the silly exploits of my husband and children. Once again, I'm not always thrilled with the picture I see; it's not the perfect one of a model on the pages of a magazine or the innocent, unblighted look of an adolescent girl, one who has yet to carry around the weight of a child for nine months and on. I yearn to be like those models and innocent girls; I want their lithe figures and unblemished skin.

Then I catch a glimpse of Brianna standing in front of the mirror, sometimes clothed, sometimes fresh out of a bathtub, wet and stark naked. She twirls around and around, gazing with rapt fascination at her reflection. She smiles in delight, interested in all of her little body's capable parts and in what they can do. She goes up close so her face is a few inches from the glass, making faces and laughing at how outrageous she can make her expressions. She feels no self-consciousness, no fear that someone is going to laugh at her or tell her she doesn't look good. She doesn't try to cover anything up or stand a certain way so that pockets of fat or loose skin are hidden from view. She just looks at what she's got and is happy with it.

I can't do that yet. But Brianna can look at me and be positive about what she sees. I stand naked briefly sometimes when I'm getting dried off and dressed after a shower, and she looks curiously at me. She remembers what my body looked like while I was carrying around her baby sister, when she would poke at my bulging, taut belly. Now she still pokes at my stomach — deflated, flaccid, and jiggly as Santa's bowl full of jelly — and observes, laughing, "You have a BIG belly!" I take it in stride. She doesn't mean her statement to be negative; it's just a fact, and it's OK. She probably thinks it's something I can be proud of, and she'll aspire to have a big belly when she's grown up too. It is my constant reminder, a proof that I made the sacrifice to bring two lives into this world.

Even now, Brianna finds some comfort in that same haven where she made her home for nine months. It provides a soft, warm pillow for her to rest her head. She made herself comfortable on my belly the other night as we read our books. I thought to myself that she wouldn't have done so if I had rock-hard abs. And I would have missed out on the closeness that we shared because my belly was so soft and inviting. It was just so snuggly.

At other times, I stand in the mirror, with nice clothes covering up my stretch marks and flabby spots, and I can forget those "imperfections" that lay beneath my fashionable camouflage. I can forget that I carry badges of honor that don't seem so honorable to the fashion world inhabited by size-two models. Brianna walks into the room, where I gaze at my reflection contentedly, and says, "Mommy, you look pretty." And I know she's right. I look pretty in clothes or out, and I feel beautiful, whether or not I'm model material. I really wouldn't trade my two beautiful, sweet girls for any perfect body.

Brianna's participation in her first Christmas amounted to eating tinsel off our tree. Her second Christmas consisted of some interest in tearing the wrapping paper off the gifts. The third evoked more delight in decorating the tree and in helping everyone else unwrap their packages. This Christmas has been most interesting to date. She showed as much eagerness to go out and get a tree as my husband did (he started chomping at the bit sometime around Thanksgiving), and she delicately and deliberately helped him place ornaments on it once we finally had it securely stationed in the corner of our dining room.

She's also started to get into the spirit of what's inside the brightly wrapped packages under that tree. A few days ago, a friend asked Brianna what she wanted for Christmas, and she matter-of-factly replied, "Presents."

Last but certainly not least, I have found Brianna is starting to understand the origin and spirit of the holiday we observe every December 25. She realizes that we are celebrating the birth of Jesus, the Savior of the world. Already she recognizes his pictures and reminds us that Jesus loves us all. To reinforce this tender recognition inside of her, I decided the first song I would teach her about Christmas, instead of "Jingle Bells" or a Santa tune (which she's already picked up somewhere anyway — probably from one of those completely annoying dancing Santas in the mall), would be "Away in a Manger."

Our elaborate — and sometimes too lengthy — bedtime ritual, in addition to bathing, going potty, brushing teeth, and reading, has evolved to include sitting on the small rocking chair in the corner of her room and singing. I found it only natural to slip my new song into our roster of "Frere Jacques" and "Hello Mr. Turkey." I sang it over and over the first night, and Brianna rocked quietly with me, listening intently. She made no real attempt to sing along, but the second night she hopped right in and had it down pat. After a few sing-alongs together, I let her take the lead, and I listened to her small, clear, pure voice intone the simple notes and lyrics. I rocked us both, cradling my quickly growing child in my arms in the low light of the room. We sang reverently, quietly, picturing the little lord Jesus asleep in his humble bed of hay.

Brianna pulled her pile of blankets close around her and observed: "Marissa has a lot of blankets. I have a lot of blankets, too. And I have a lot of toys to play with and books to read. Mommy and Daddy have books to read, too. And I can go to the day care and play with my friends and go to their houses..." She listed a number of the conveniences and enjoyments she has. I was amazed at her insight to all of her blessings. I listened and responded that yes, she was very blessed, very lucky.

As I put her in her bed, Brianna insisted on having a reprise of "Away in a Manger." As the song concluded once again, she asked, "Baby Jesus didn't have a bed?" No, sweetie, he didn't. The greatest person to be born on this earth came into humble circumstances, without even a crib to sleep in. And here my firstborn was safe and warm in our own home, in a bed piled with comforters handmade by dear friends. The central heating system was churning out temperature-controlled air from a vent on the floor, the electric nightlight and halogen lamp were casting a pale yellow glow across the room so my flesh and blood wouldn't be scared in the dark.

The maturing body's cells were multiplying at astounding rates, thanks to ample food and a nightly dose of milk. Her brain's synapses and neurons were firing constantly, allowing her to learn from everything around her, including the toys and the shelves full of books. Her hair and skin were clean and smelling fresh from her dip into a tub full of soap and hot water, gleaned from an almost mystical source, pipes full of never-ending, clean water.

Her clothes were new, warm, and even cute, fitting her

just perfectly and setting off her natural beauty. They were in a huge supply, plenty of pajamas and socks and shoes and day-time clothes, enough to go a couple of weeks without doing wash.

Her voice promises to develop into a pleasing instrument, thanks to inherited musical talent from both Mom and Dad, all of us blessed by our maker with individual and enjoyable gifts. Her oft-repeated songs, now "Away in a Manger" among them, lilt with gladness and confidence, a smooth, adorable child soprano. Melodies are unmistakable, the words clearly articulated, the meanings understood to the singer.

In that blessed room with my own little gift from heaven, I sat suspended in time. The soft light in the room and the spirit in the air took me back to that first Christmas. I could almost see by the light of a bright new star in the heavens, I could hear the cooing of a tiny new child, I could feel the impact of that special birth and the life and death that would follow. I hugged my own child, kissed her soft forehead, and tucked her into her bed for the night. I looked at her angelic face as her eyes closed and she prepared to sleep, and I thought of the ability she had to count her blessings. My mind and heart were moved, and I counted my blessings too.

PART IV
FULL HEART – MEMORIES

CHAPTER 9
NOW IS A MEMORY

My earliest memories seem to start around the time I was three or four. I remember racing into my parents' bedroom with my sister when I was probably three and a half years old; we would greet every new day with them, from what I can guess. My mother would always say, "Oh, good morning, Cathy!" Apparently, my sister Christine called me "Oh" or "Oh-ee" at that time (she was about a year to a year and a half old then); my mom figures Chris condensed the beginning and end of that whole phrase down to an easy name for me.

I remember visiting my grandparents around that same age, when they lived in a high-rise apartment building in town. Once, I somehow managed to leave the building and get locked out. I can picture myself outside that tall city-block building running from locked door to locked door in a vain attempt to get back inside the building. How that was resolved, I don't remember, and I suspect my parents don't remember the whole situation at all, but apparently it turned out OK because I'm still around today. In that same apartment, I remember my uncle showing me how to tie my shoelaces. I remember my grandmother's neighbor down the hall giving me a handmade Snoopy pillow and a stuffed monkey that now sits, worn and tattered as much as the fabled

Velveteen Rabbit, among my daughter's collection. I remember the food I ate there: cantaloupe, alphabet soup, and Nilla wafers that sat high up on a pantry shelf but not necessarily out of my reach (my mom shakes her head ruefully every time she recalls how accomplished — and dangerous — a climber I was).

I vividly recall the Baskin-Robbins that was down the street from that well-secured apartment building: my grandparents took me there enough that I was very familiar with its location. My grandmother likes to tell me how I would lean in the direction of that Baskin-Robbins anytime we'd drive near it. I can even now picture how it looked from my three-foot-high vantage point, horizontal refrigerators showcasing the large buckets of ice cream just above where my eyes could see unassisted, and how it smelled, of cones and sauces and gallon upon gallon of thirty-one flavors of sweet creamy heaven, and of many other blended scents I could never identify but which together made an undeniable, unique aroma. I like to go in those shops now, not just because of the obvious fact that I could live on ice cream (hey, it has calcium — I don't think I'll have a problem with osteoporosis), but because that unique smell and atmosphere is exactly the same all these years later, honestly making me feel like a kid again.

The memories pile up in my head in thousands of downy, comforting layers, like soft flannel sheets on the bed of the Princess and the Pea. I enjoy hopping in to the middle of the layers and savoring a scoop of ice cream from that Baskin-Robbins or a warm spring day in one of our old houses out in the country. One house in which my family lived was on top of a Pennsylvania mountain; the view of the other rolling mountains, covered with trees and farms, was spectacular. Another house was an old, rambling home that sat on a most-

ly unused farm. We rented the house, so we didn't feed animals or pick crops, but we children had run of the seemingly
endless acres of mostly fallow fields and grassy meadows. One
of my most soothing, cherished still-life memory pictures is of
lying in the middle of a large field of tall, green grass, spread
out comfortably, staring straight up at the blue sky dotted
with wisps of white clouds, and hearing the gentle drone of
distant airplanes. When I am stressed and caught up in the fast
pace of daily work, I try to take a moment to picture that
scene and recapture the tranquility and utter lack of worry and
care that I felt that time as a child.

I took my husband on a grand tour of these idyllic spots
where I lived my formative years. We loaded the kids in a rented car and drove north on a pilgrimage. I traipsed around the
countryside of Pennsylvania, pulling along my young family
to see every house and every town I lived in over the course of
about five years. It was a lot of driving — including our stops
to see historical sites and friends and relatives, we logged almost
three thousand miles — but it was worth it. Much was just the
same as I remembered it — the house on the mountain looked
just the same; the rocky, steep, dirt roads were just as narrow
and winding and slow going as before; the scenery was the
same except less visible because the trees had grown taller,
obstructing the view. The boon-docks locations were still just
as much in the boonies as I remember, but more so in a way
because I've lived in big cities since then, so the distance and
remoteness of those days is even more shocking to me now.

We drove to one city just to get a look at the beautiful university campus where my dad taught and got his doctoral
degree, and my husband drove around at my direction, as I
tried to navigate us from my long-unused memory of streets
and landmarks. I was very proud of myself for taking us out

on the edge of town straight to our neat old farmhouse, which was so old the bathroom had been fashioned out of a bedroom because bathrooms were simply outhouses in the day it was built, and its lack of real closets required me to have an armoire. This old house was the setting for my filed-away freeze-frames of celebrating several Easters and birthdays and being told I was too young to play Monopoly yet. From this house I clearly remember nights when I was too frightened of monsters hiding under my bed to be able to leap over them to reach my parents' bedroom down the hall — I learned that I'd better stop reading my school library's books about classic horror films. It was probably this experience that convinced me that I'd better never actually *watch* a horror film, since even the books *about* the films scared the heck out of me. I think the only true scary flick I've seen since then, aside from Hitchcock movies, is one of the *Nightmare on Elm Street* series because a boyfriend in high school forced me to watch it. I don't plan to watch any others.

That rickety farmhouse, which holds so many little memories and the genesis of my determination to avoid horror flicks, in whose giant, sloping backyard I saw a Goodyear blimp at very close range and lazed languidly staring at the sky, is gone. The yard — the fields, the pastures, the tall grass and barns, the tree in front that had been split in half by lightning and which had blocked traffic on the road for a few hours, thus making our address a landmark — and the house itself are completely gone, as if they never existed. I drove past the site with my husband and two daughters and made my husband double back three times (I know he was getting tired of this). I was trying to convince myself that I was mistaken on the site, on the address, but I realized after the third or fourth pass that it must be gone. In the place of those idyllic scenes of my childhood is just a large, leveled patch of dirt, being readied for a subdivision of new, dull, cookie-cutter houses with modern bathrooms and walk-in closets, probably each with a small, square, flat, boring yard. The slate was wiped clean.

I felt like a part of me had been killed. My memories were bulldozed. I had wanted to share with my husband the stage on which took place the many acts of a play in my mind, in some childlike fantasy that he then magically would be able to glimpse some of those very scenes coming to life. I wanted so much for him to see the beautiful scenery and to feel those same emotions that remain in my heart, remnants of those long-ago, personal events. I wanted to relive those events myself, not by turning back the clock, but by simply standing on the stage. But my stage was gone. It felt like Brigadoon had disappeared, leaving me with only the memory of its existence for one day in my childhood, and a lingering tune of merriment on MacConnachy Square. I was crushed.

Since then, I have recovered. Nothing has really changed for me now that I am back in my adult life, taking care of my home and my family, teaching my little children. I still have my memories; the fact that the site where they were created is now irrevocably changed means nothing to my heart and my mind. The warm, cozy memories are still locked away and are still accessible for the days in which I need to lounge in them, to bask in that warm spring sun.

What I've also realized is that the memories are just beginning for my daughter. My memories begin at about the age she is now. As I reflect on those days of wonder from my childhood, it hits me that those days are *now* for her. She's creating her memories; I'm helping. What strikes me is that any moment may be a lasting memory for her — the mornings when she runs into my bedroom pronouncing joyously, "I'm awake!"; the moments she points out pretty flowers to me outside the gym; the rainbows and bunny rabbits we spy from our front steps; the trips to the local Baskin-Robbins. Will she lean toward the ice cream shops when we drive by them? Will she tell me one day, "My fondest memories are of eating drippy mint-chocolate-chip cones while you fed small bites of your cones to Marissa, in that Baskin-Robbins that was turned into a tattoo parlor"? Who knows what she will remember. My most fond, striking memories are not those that my parents would have expected to emerge as the stand-outs; they are not the carefully-engineered vacations or sightseeing excursions. They're the little day-to-day experiences that just happened serendipitously and whimsically.

I try to remind myself that Brianna's memories are today, that they're being gathered every moment, etched into her brain forever, not to be blotted out or bulldozed. I try to make every day a good memory for my daughter; I teach her and read to her and try to be patient as she teaches me what she sees. I think back on my memories and the treasures they hold and realize that she will one day look back and smile on these days, wishing she could return to them, feeling that no time was ever better than what we're living right now.

CHAPTER 10
SEASONS

Since I spent the first ten years of my life in Pennsylvania, I was familiar with four full seasons, and I would like my own children to have some of that same experience, to feel the vast differences between the poles of weather. The winters are snowy and cold, the summers warm and muggy. Springtimes are lavishly green and filled with budding flowers and trees; autumns are bedecked with bright reds and oranges, garishly splashed on every tree and mountainside. I enjoyed each of the seasons for the opportunities for play they presented. Winter, with its snow and icy slopes, offered spectacular amateur sporting opportunities. Since my parents always found us homes placed on huge plots of land, graced with hills and wide meadows, we had ready-made frozen amusement parks on our own property each cold season.

My mom properly bundled up each small child every day as we bounced around her, hopping around like little Mexican jumping beans asking to be freed from the confinements of a boring heated house. We first donned thermal underwear, then a couple of layers of pants and shirts, then gloves and hats, then plastic pants and waterproof coats. The warm, snowtight boots were the final touch to the practical ensemble. Each layer was securely fastened and checked for watertightness, as if we were entering a quarantined government area contaminated with virulent gases or deadly bacteria. When we were cleared for entry to the cold outdoors, my mother helped us lumber out into the virgin, unspotted white wilderness, a vast canvas waiting for us to turn it into art. We were so well layered and bundled that we walked a bit like mummies or zombies, lurching unsteadily with outstretched, immobile limbs. I know we were an amusing sight for my parents.

Our vast canvas, filled with an abundance of white raw material for our art, provided us endless opportunities for sculpture, painting, and not-so-graceful sporting events. Pennsylvania was cold enough and northern enough that it received bounteous snow every winter, coating it with several feet of flaky precipitation. I remember our car being fully buried by the stuff, forcing my father to dig it out every day, largely thanks to wind drifting on the side of the road. The snow was endless and plentiful and beautiful. I enjoyed the pristine look of it at the beginning of the day and the knowledge that we would never run out of material for our daily creative endeavors. After a few hours, we would be forced to come inside not because the supply was depleted but because the cold had finally worked its way through our numerous protective layers.

We could pile it up in huge mounds and jump into it, much like we did with leaves in the fall. It was soft and downy. Some winters the snow was a bit wetter and icier, making it ideal for our slicker sports. One house we lived in had a fantastic natural park behind it, created by a rocky hill. When that hill was coated with snow, we could coax curvy, steep, slick slides from its face, between the strategically placed rocks, and breeze speedily from top to bottom. We could also speed all the way down the mountain's dirt road on our one prop, a generous-sized sled, which made for an incredible roller-coaster-type ride, but we didn't take advantage of this option very often because climbing all the way back up with that sled in tow took back-breaking effort, not necessarily worth the short-lived but exhilarating thrill.

I particularly enjoyed the wetter snow some years, although it more quickly penetrated our layers of clothing defenses than the drier, fluffier variety, because it made for great forts. With my mittened hands, I would pack the snow into sturdy foot-high walls and trenches. When I was particularly industrious, I could make a huge complex of walls and doors, the rooms and buildings creating a community that stretched across our large yard. The result looked somewhat like a garden maze seen from the top or like the numerous unroofed, squat-walled apartment buildings left behind by the Anasazi in the Southwest, in Chaco Canyon or Mesa Verde. I was always proud of my detailed networks of foot-high rooms, which were much like the architectural sketches I created for myself indoors from pencil, paper and rulers. But unlike the Anasazis' enduring mud creations, my beautiful buildings were just a memory when more snow buried them or the warmth of spring turned them into water gushing down the mountainsides in cold streams.

In addition to sledding and making forts, we could fall back on the time-honored traditions of making snowmen or snow angels. Angels were easy and quick; we cast our layered bodies onto the virgin white earth, spread our arms wide, and flapped up and down to create beautiful wings. Since these were created so quickly and readily, our large yards were covered with three sizes of angels. We also made snowmen with carefully rolled large balls of snow, stacking them and decorating them the best we could with pieces of sticks or rocks we could salvage from beneath the coating of white. Of course, many of the balls never realized their potential as snowmen's torsos because they were thrown at siblings, splintering into icy pieces on a back, an arm, or even a twisted-up, crying, exposed red face.

My parents had similar experiences as children growing up with snow. They both lived in the North, where the snow is a constant, expected every winter. My father was just reading me a letter he wrote to his father when he was a child attending a military school. It was wintertime, and the school sat on a large, beautiful hill, perfect for sledding. My father wrote "Will you please bring the sled this weekend when you visit? The hill is covered in snow." The snow and playing in it is my family's heritage.

My husband, on the other hand, was born in the tropical Philippines, which is generally warm and very humid, experiencing torrential rain as its primary precipitation, at least in the more southern part that was home to his family. He lived there only a year and a half before his parents brought him and his brother and sister to sunny California. Even Northern California, where he grew up, is not exactly known for its snow.

My husband tells me that his father actually took the children on some pilgrimages east toward the Sierras, where snow was more likely to be found. One year they drove and drove, deeper into the mountains, but still never saw a trace of snow. Another year was more successful, and my husband and his siblings were able to throw a few snowballs. But it was still just an exotic treat, much like importing dried tropical fruit from the Philippines to the States for expatriates craving something different than the duller domestic apples or peaches.

With this heritage, the years of playful winters in my blood, I wondered if my daughters would inherit any of it. My girls were born in Alabama, where snow is much like a displaced Yankee — not terribly common, and infrequent and foreign enough to be unsettling. Large storm systems here in the South send natives into a panic, and they raid stores for milk, bread, and propane stoves. They even stock up on videos to keep them busy when they find themselves stranded at home because of a half-inch of fluff on the roads. The schools promptly close the moment a storm is imminent, and everyone retreats to the safety of their houses. Frankly, these Southerners are not used to snow and they're not prepared for it. And they're certainly not used to getting to play in the snow; they have no plastic pants or waterproof gloves and boots and no sleds.

Sadly, I realize this is the case with my own daughters. They have coats but nothing else geared for snow play. They haven't needed snow pants or heavy, waterproof gloves, so why should I invest in expensive equipment like that, even if it were to be stocked in local stores? A few months before Brianna's fourth birthday, a big storm swept through the East, particularly surprising and stalling the South and the East Coast. It threatened to forestall the Super Bowl, horror of horrors. The South flew into a frenzy of hasty preparation, clearing shelves of milk and videos.

I was not too worried about the driving conditions or slick roads since I have experience driving in the snow. Rather, I was a little excited because this storm meant that my daughters would finally see snow. The last good storm we saw while living here in Alabama was when I was pregnant with Brianna, so she didn't really get to see much of the white precipitation from her cozy, windowless womb. Then winter after winter, we either were in California or in a snow-less Alabama. Almost four years old, with a heritage of snow, and still not a glimpse of it, let alone a tumble in a big pile of it.

The night the storm was supposed to strike, I tucked Brianna into bed with a promise that tomorrow she could play in the snow. Her face lit up, and she eagerly asked if she would be able to make a snowman. I told her she might. She only knows snowmen from picture books or the Charlie Brown Christmas video. How sad! But I was happy to tell her she would see it for herself and maybe make a snowman with her own two hands.

The next morning, the forecasters proved to be right. I looked out my bedroom window and saw a thin blanket of snow covering our yard and those of our neighbors'. Brianna ran into my room and peeked out too, and the sight of such strange stuff elicited some oohs and ahhs, and most notably a plea to go out and play in it. I wasn't eager to pack off my warm-blooded, unprotected daughter off into the cold at 8 in the morning, so I told her we would go to the gym and she could play in the snow when we got back home. She accepted this surprisingly readily, and we trooped off to exercise.

At 11 A.M., I walked out the front door of the gym with my two girls in tow. No more white blanket; it had disappeared, and the weather was surprisingly warm. I was stunned into pausing for a moment to double-check on the situation. No, I saw no sign of that magical white dust resting anywhere on the road or the parking lot or the dead brown grass. And another pair of eyes had witnessed the same sad phenomenon. I heard an intake of breath and a disappointed little voice protesting, "The snow's gone!" I looked over at my little girl, whose face had fallen as low as the bare ground on which she stood. I have never seen her look sadder or more pitiful. I was crestfallen as well and surprised beyond measure. My heart broke for her. I couldn't believe what had happened and was disappointed in myself for letting her down. We pulled ourselves together and went home.

I hoped on the short drive to our house that remnants of the storm would still be visible on our lawn, and as the car climbed the hill, I crossed my fingers and hoped beyond hope, for the sake of my little child's dreams to play in the snow. Sure enough, when we pulled into the driveway, a few patches of white remained on the lawn, around the trees and in front of our sidewalk. I took Marissa inside, since she was too young to experience sub-sixty-degree temperatures for more than a dash between the climate-controlled car and house, and allowed Brianna to don a pair of my large gloves to prepare her for playing in the tiny patch of snow. She happily marched around in the small circles of white, mere fractions of the large, pristine expanses I encountered as a child, making footprints on the two- or three-foot-diameter canvases. She walked around and around, leaving red, clayey marks in her wake. She picked up some snow in her hands and felt its coldness, its almost-sugary texture, comprised of almost undetectable flakes of ice, not quite large enough to be sharp. She made little balls of it. She seemed content with what fate had dealt her, and she stayed outside for about fifteen minutes in the pitiful amount of snow that was left for her. She came inside, cheeks a little rosy, hands a bit cold, and shoes lightly coated in red mud, not well bundled or covered with wet snow, but happy that she was finally able to experience the magic of snow.

As crestfallen as she was when we saw the dry ground outside the gym, Brianna rebounded quickly. I was impressed because it was entirely possible she would pout or cry or fall on the floor in frustration and disappointment, her crankiness clouding my day. But no, she accepted what she had and made the most of it. I can't say I've always done that when presented with less than what I had hoped for. But I can say that I will always keep in my memory the picture of my sweet daughter cheerfully making footprints in a square foot of snow, the disappointment forgotten and the reality of the present accepted and enjoyed.

So the snow is in scarce supply here, the winter season merely being one in which the heat is gone and the trees and lawns are stripped of their green coats. Summer takes up a large part of the year, heating and humidifying all creation until fall mercifully comes and blends quickly into that snow-less winter. But springtime is still glorious, in the South now, as well as in the North of my memories. And in both places I enjoy and have enjoyed lilacs and the ubiquitous curtains of delicate, fragrant wisteria. I don't know much about horticulture, but they seem like cousins to me, similar enough that the wisteria can stand in as a memory stunt double.

So whatever you label them, these beautiful and strong-smelling flowers always stimulate a swarm of memories for me, on a variety of sensual levels. That rickety but fascinating old house in Pennsylvania that has now been cleared away to make room for a new, generic, history-free home sported a glorious lilac bush in its spacious side yard. Not only was this bush beautifully outfitted in delicate lavender-hued petals and graced with an intoxicating fragrance, but its squarish, hollow frame created a natural fort, perfect for the fantastical reveries of a young girl.

I remember many times putting my hands through the purple mass and popping open a secret "door" of branches and flowers. I would slip in through the small opening, the branches popping back into place immediately, sealing me in like the door of the holodeck on *Star Trek*, where I found myself inside an unbroken cave of blooming wonders. Springtime was delightful, as I could sit inside and think and dream, drenched in the heady perfume of lilac. I was truly in another world, almost outside of time, where anything was possible to my young, blossoming imagination.

Twenty-plus years later, I eagerly look forward to spring, particularly to the advent of the lilacs. They aren't around for long, so I appreciate them during their short but magnificent tenure. I lived in the West for a few years and saw nary a bloom, so since I've moved back East, I've reveled even deeper in my lilac time travel. In the South, I've reveled in these thick curtains of wisteria, allowing them to link me to my childhood lilac fancies.

When I'm lucky and conditions are right, these flowers climb up everywhere, taking over and acting rather pesky for other people's more controlled tastes, but I want to bow down at their feet and bury my face in their majesty. Their intense, paradisiacal aroma (so strong an onslaught it creates nearly a tangible wall, like the perimeter of a department-store perfume section) takes me right back to my childhood, so that I feel anything is possible and everything is right with the world, that my fantasies can come true. They're healing. I believe in aromatherapy.

My daughter seems to have picked up the scent. She has no emotional connections to lilacs and maybe never will, unless she later recalls her mother's unusual fondness for the flowers. But she enjoys any blossom, be it weed or carefully cultivated award-winner, that she runs into. Since it is spring as I write this, she has lots of opportunities to smell the flowers. And, I am ashamed to admit, more opportunities than I'd like to indulge her with. Everywhere we go, more flowers stand in our way as we try to get to our destinations, seemingly tripping us up and trapping us with invisible vines. My gym has a large array of flowers and plants along its front wall, and we must walk down the floral receiving line every day as we get out of the car and make our way toward the front door. Most of the time, I am very much looking forward to depositing my two daughters in the nursery for an hour or so of time to myself and another opportunity to work off my pregnancy fat. Therefore, I am ashamed to say that time on a treadmill seems more important than time spent smelling and otherwise appreciating beautiful flowers.

Brianna, as always, ignores my need to get a move-on, and she goes about her own business. Her routine is to step out of the car, run toward the beginning of the reception line, and stop at the first and figuratively shake hands and exchange lengthy and protracted greetings, probably asking after the flower's grandmother, second cousin, great-niece, and third cousin's hairdresser. She stands at attention, looks at the flowers, glances at me, and turns back to the flowers, giving them an elaborate stage sniff. When she is satisfied that I have given an equally appreciative sniff, she inches forward one step to the next plant and repeats the process. As soon as we have both inhaled the scent of each pansy, iris, and gladiolus, we are then free to move on into the gym, where she can play with the toys and day-care workers.

At first I was annoyed with this whole process. Being a mother who's home all day with my children, I grasp at any opportunity for time alone like a hypothermic, starving, drowning woman overboard clings to a lifeline cast out from a cruise liner, but I realized that this routine was inevitable and really would only slightly delay that time alone, so I might as well get with the program and enjoy it, or else be angry and annoyed day in and day out, on schedule. I make sure now I have enough time (just a few extra minutes) so that I don't have to rush my daughter into the gym each day, and we smell the flowers.

It's scarcely a hardship for me. The flowers are looking brighter and more plentiful each day, and it's relaxing to put myself in the moment and enjoy what they have to offer. There they stand in their best dress, a floral wedding every day, and most everyone else is passing right by, in a hurry to go inside a stuffy, labyrinth-like old building with lots of metal-and-plastic equipment and sweaty bodies. Thanks to Brianna, I'm enjoying what they are offering, a lovely face and a delicious perfume, and I carry their fragrance with me as I proceed through my smelly, salty workout.

CHAPTER 11
SEEING A RAINBOW IN A BANANA

Countless baby-magazine articles and "what-to-expect" books on parenting confidently inform millions of parents severely lacking in baby information that an infant doesn't have clear eyesight at birth; the tiny miracle that is a newborn only sees well at a distance of about a foot, from where she is nursing to her mother's face. Everything else is fuzzy. Reportedly, the baby's eyesight improves steadily up until about age two, when she can see clearly at all distances, much like any adult who doesn't require eyeglasses — twenty-twenty.

From my own experience with Brianna, I am convinced that eyesight is perfect — perhaps even supernormal, something like four hundred-twenty — by around age three, for she has proved to me on countless occasions that she is capable of seeing much more than I can.

For instance, a few months before Brianna turned three, we took her and her seven-month-old sister on a trip to Disney World. During long jaunts such as this one, they both required frequent snacks, more than would be necessary with all the diversions available at home. One of the snack/diversions I handed back to her from my position in the front seat of the monotony-mobile was a banana. A split-second later (get it — banana split?) I was hailed by my ravenous child, not for more food, but for an observation, before she devoured her prey. She waved the nutritious yellow fruit (notice it wasn't a sugar-laden lollipop or cupcake) at me and crowed, "Look, Mommy! A rainbow!"

She smiled winningly, her face lit up by excitement at her discovery, and I absent-mindedly thought to myself as the road stretched on ahead of us, "Sure, that's great, honey, you're doing great on the shape, but it's not exactly multi-colored." But no sooner had that thought passed through my mind than another paraded through: she knows exactly what it IS; she is just looking a little deeper. Her eyesight was functioning quite well, as those baby articles had informed me it would at her age, but her vision was allowing her to see levels invisible to the naked eye.

I saw that banana too, the perfect curve of its form, the half-moon shape truly reminiscent of a rainbow, but I saw no rainbow. My vision, as well as my eyesight, had deteriorated long since age three. My daughter's wise observation acted like a pair of childhood glasses, and when I looked through those glasses instead of brushing them aside, adult-like and all business, I saw in my memory the most vivid rainbow I've ever laid eyes on.

That rainbow happened during the period we lived in the old house on the top of a small northern-Appalachian mountain, a precarious perch reachable only by rocky dirt roads, barely navigable during wintertime when freshly and slickly paved by ice and snow. The house and its spacious environs were in the middle of nowhere, and the rough road surely would have done damage to our car if it hadn't already been beat up, but the home's high-up location afforded a breathtaking view. During the summer we could see the other mountains and valleys, rolling hills covered with countless leafy trees, creating from a distance the appearance of a lumpy but incredibly soft green patchwork quilt. In autumn, the same hills were awash in color, brilliant reds, oranges, and yellows lighting up the hillsides. We may have been ridiculously far from a shopping mall or skyscraper, but what we got to see every day made up for our lack of easy access to civilization — at least so I felt then.

On my tenth birthday, the ordinary view became extraordinary. It had rained a little but the sun had come out, shining brilliantly through the mist still hanging in the air. Someone in my family (most likely my mother) looked out the window and spied a rainbow. It was a double bow and intensely bright and large, showing us all the colors of the spectrum in all their glory not just once but twice. Each colored curve was clearly defined, from tip to tip, stretching from one valley to another. We could see one end particularly well, the spectrum of colors blending together somehow into a gleaming yellow circle way down in the crook of the valleys — it actually did look like a pot of gold. My family and I stood in a group and admired it, all ahush. The moment froze in time for me, the brightness of that rainbow searing its image onto the photo paper of my consciousness, ready for easy retrieval anytime I see a rainbow, no matter how pale or puny, today. Even if I just catch a glimpse of a shaft of light being split raggedly and weakly by a small stream of water from a garden hose, I remember that birthday and its glory. The two separate events along the time continuum temporarily merge in a misty double-exposure of colorful light.

So even though I am still able to retrieve that memory, I only do so when prodded by another rainbow. No other visual stimulus triggers that chain reaction of neurons in my brain that leads to that colorful memory. But my daughter's youthful ability to look beyond the superficial allowed me to see a rainbow in a mere potassium-laden snack, as we drove down a seemingly endless, gray highway toward a more enjoyable destination.

Brianna has demonstrated this Superman-like eyesight for me countless times in the months since she first showed me the rainbow in the banana. I have been reminded to recognize the extraordinary in the ordinary things every day by a three-year-old with remarkable vision and insight. The vision she so easily and naturally enjoys has helped me to regenerate my own vision, deteriorated slightly since I was age three, but not irreversibly damaged. My little girl is my set of eyeglasses on the world, and it is amazingly bright and beautiful, colorful and full of variety like that rainbow.

Speaking of seeing clearly, only a year or two after my seminal childhood rainbow experience, my literal eyesight went downhill seemingly overnight. One day everything seemed normal, and the next I realized that things weren't quite right. I was actually sitting in church the moment I realized that my peepers weren't functioning at top capacity. You could say I had a revelation, but what really happened was that I looked toward the front of the chapel, expecting to see the page number for our next congregational hymn, and only made out a white and black blur in the place the numbers were supposed to be posted. I turned to my dad and gave my assessment: "I think I need glasses."

My mom took me to the eye doctor. We strolled in and had all the usual tests ("Does *A* or *B* look better? *A* or *B*? One or two?", all of which is very annoying because the slight difference in the two is always such a tough *judgment call;* you figure if you guess wrong you'll end up with an expensive pair of glasses that don't even work), confirming that, sure enough, I was nearsighted. I had the excitement of getting to pick out my very first pair of glasses. A few years before, I had visited the eye doctor and found to my disappointment that my eyes were just fine, so I wouldn't be able to wear neat glasses like my mom; however, at age ten, despite being intrigued by the newness of it all, I was probably a little less than thrilled with the glamorous options available to me. My chosen frames were pink-tinted plastic, somewhat clunky and large, but so were everyone else's in 1980.

When the proper prescription had been placed in my frames and my mom and I were summoned to pick them up, I allowed the technician on duty to adjust them to my face and clean them up and bend and twist them just so. I don't remember how I perceived their cosmetic effects on my face, but I vividly remember how it felt to look through them. I was floored. As soon as the frames were placed for good over my deficient windows to the world, I was astounded at how clear and bright everything looked.

Driving home, I looked out at the landscape like a time-traveler awed by the miracles surrounding me. Only I wasn't gawking at the horseless carriages speeding by or the huge multi-purpose enclosed markets. I was staring at the ground, the grass in particular. I could see *every single blade of grass,* not just a lime-tinted stretch of homogeneous turf. When I gazed at the trees, I saw individual, colorful quivering leaves, instead of a big lumpy blur of green. I think before I got my glasses, I envisioned trees as kindergartners do — as brown sticks with a squiggly circle of green crayon perched on top. Through my newly acquired clunky plastic frames, I saw the branches, large limbs and small spreading out in uneven yet somehow sym-metrical patterns, each tiny branch hosting a number of deli-cately-shaped leaves, unique as snowflakes. I never took those leaves or the crowded patches of grass blades for granted again.

At this point, Brianna still has sharp eyesight. I doubt that this will last, if my understanding of basic genetics is right. My eyesight isn't too great; I am banned from driving without cor-rective lenses. My husband's vision is twice as bad as mine. His lenses, even made from the so-called thinner, lighter material, are thick, heavy and clunky. We're quite the pair. I feel sure that Brianna will be sitting in an optometrist's chair easily by the time she is ten. But for now she can see perfectly fine.

The reason I am positive about the quality of her vision is that she can pick anything out a mile away. She has noticed cute little lap dogs at fifty yards away, birds, cats, whatever is interesting to her. I particularly got a kick out of an observa-tion she made when we were driving to her two-day-a-week day care. We were stopped in the turn lane, straddling four lanes of traffic, waiting to take a left. Being the responsible driver, I was naturally watching (very carefully) the speeding oncoming cars, waiting like a cat about to pounce on a juicy mouse for my chance to make a dash for the other side through any slight break in the solid traffic. But from the back seat, I heard Brianna urgently announce that she saw a brush. With anything she says that she feels is of any importance, she expects an immediate and interested response. I glanced about hurriedly and not very thoroughly, trying to figure out where in the world she was seeing a brush, of all things. After she gave me some pointers, I observed smack to our left, just a few feet away, a little round hairbrush stuck in the top of a reflec-tor marker in the median. She was right — what a weird place for someone to have put a brush!

We remarked to each other all the way up the street and into the center about how funny it was to see a brush in the road. Every single time we went that same way, Brianna confirmed to me that the brush was still there, until one day recently, it was gone, as mysteriously as it had appeared. Maybe one of the inmates who do prison-release cleanups along the roadway was having a bad-hair day and stumbled onto a serendipitous find. Who knows?

What struck me was how easy it is to miss stuff like that, seeing something really unusual in a usual place, or something banal in an atypical setting. Many of us miss out completely on the funny or sad incongruities of life because we're simply not looking. A four-headed dog could walk by us on the street, and we'd pay more attention to its owner's hairstyle or brand of blue jeans — and that's if we're looking up from our cell phone/CD player/sausage biscuit. Brianna doesn't miss a beat. If it's strange, she sees it. If it's completely normal, she sees it.

It's all a matter of perspective. Without my glasses, I had no idea what I was missing. Three years before, my vision had been perfectly normal and I could see the blades of grass and the individual leaves on the trees. But my vision slowly deteriorated, going at such a deceptive pace that I had no idea what I was losing. Soon enough, I pictured a tree as a big green blob on a brown stick. My daughter is still young enough to be interested in the seemingly common, plain, dull world around her. She's probably not seen everything yet, but she's still interested in things she's already seen. They're not yet old news. Not just once have I been filling up the car with gas, staring at the pump's numbers climb ever higher or hasting to wash the windows, when Brianna has excitedly cried out, "Look — a bird!" I look around at eye level, or even down on the ground, seeing nothing, expecting she's just imagining things again (as she is, admittedly, often apt to do), when she points out to me that a few birds are congregating on the roof of the convenience mart.

It's still easy for Brianna; her job is to explore the world, discover what it has to offer her, wherever she might be. She has few pressures or external expectations. She can closely look around her at every detail, gazing up at the sky, looking carefully down at the ground, playing the role of a brave explorer in an exotic new locale. Her studied, professional eye rakes the landscape, absorbing all of the information and filing it away in her personal databank. She would be a poor adventurer indeed if she allowed herself to miss anything because of distractions or a lack of thoroughness. She sees all and appreciates all.

We adults have grown bored with the world around us, caught up in the hectic lives we lead, focusing only on the next appointment or the seemingly important task at hand. Our heads stay at eye level, only taking in a mere ten percent of our surroundings, in a brief sweep of the landscape. Our eyes take in the light emanating from a brush in a reflector on the road but our brains, too busy with other calculations, or just tired from our life's explorations, don't even register the information. The mundane things that do register in our minds get nary a second thought, our childlike curiosity and interest stamped out over years, our inner explorers imprisoned and replaced by efficient machines. But those explorers can be coaxed out and given meaningful work again; they never die. I have found that my curiosity, though not at center stage as it was when I was a child, is still alive and well, if I nourish it and allow it room to wander free. I just have to start looking around, observing the details, the little pieces that make up the big, obvious picture.

Just a few weeks ago, I was at the dentist. The hygienist gently cleaned my teeth, asked a few (generally) yes-or-no questions, gave me some advice on dental health. Then she stepped out for a moment, leaving me alone with my bib, mouthwash, and little sink. I could easily have lain there, waiting impatiently for her return, for the removal of my bib and my liberation from the chair. Instead, I glanced over to my left and saw that her bank of instruments was in clear view and just crying out for a little close inspection. So I sat up and started exploring, wondering how each tool worked and how they worked together. I examined the different types of tips on each pen-like tool attached by tubing to the master set of controls. I noticed there were on/off switches and other mysterious switches regulating perhaps the speed or the choice of tools. (Frankly, I've already forgotten some of what I discovered and it's only been a few weeks.) I giggled a bit inwardly, thinking of myself as a renegade, an explorer venturing into off-limits territory. (This shows a bit of my personality — if I were really a fearless warrior, I'd have actually touched and played with the tools, instead of merely looking closely.) I actually felt I learned a little something, or at the very least got an idea of what it's like to be the person doing the cleaning, instead of being the clean-ee. By paying attention to the details, I gained a new perspective.

I don't always limit my curiosity to unobtrusive, quiet observations. I ask questions, too, if the need arises. A month ago at a nearby grocery store, I observed a strange little notice on my cashier's computer screen: "Have you seen Bob?" It was a simply typed, small strip of paper taped underneath the viewable area where the items scanned popped up and registered as funny abbreviations with corresponding dollar amounts. My curiosity piqued, I cast my eyes further around me and saw exact duplicates of this notice tacked to each lane's register, same place. Suspecting the query's object did not refer to a most-wanted killer or even a bad check writer, I asked the young lady on the other (official) side of the scanner what it meant. She was all too happy to inform me it was to remind all cashiers to check the bottom of every customer's cart to make sure items were not leaving the store un-paid for. (I am sure if they employed three-year-olds — who as already mentioned look up, down, and everywhere, missing nothing — that little laser-printed sign would be completely unnecessary.) I can only assume the management didn't care to shout out this problem blatantly to the customers, choosing to thinly code the employee reminder. I found the message and the situation amusing, as well as the fact that I easily cracked their little secret code. But I would have missed out on a good excuse for human interaction and a little chuckle if I hadn't looked closely.

Despite my advancing adulthood and level of responsibility, I've frankly always felt I've managed to maintain a healthy curiosity and attention to detail; I just like to look at the little things and find out what they mean. Part of it was my journalistic background; we reporters and editors are paid to ask questions, look at the details, observe incongruities. But a larger chunk of it was just a desire to keep a fresh view of the world around me.

A few weeks ago Brianna asked for one of her blankets, referring to it as "the one with the stars on it," and I honestly didn't know at first which one she meant. I just knew it was the one that was predominantly yellow. I'd completely forgotten that the reason for that was its abundance of yellow stars. So I was reminded again that I have a long ways to go toward being really observant. But Brianna has rubbed off on me, and my time spent with her in day-to-day life has really revealed the world afresh to me.

With Brianna at my side, I've laughed at a brush being stuck by someone with either a sense of humor or an ignorance of the existence of trash cans into a road reflector; I've examined microscopic tears in the paper of a cherished book or little scratches in the curve of an elbow; I've looked into the brightest, deepest, most alert and eager brown eyes I've ever had the pleasure to help create. It's pretty easy to remember to look at the details even when I'm not being guided by the master three-year-old explorer, but not quite as fun when she's not around.

CHAPTER 12
IMAGINING TOGETHER

Right before Brianna turned three, we trundled her and her baby sister off to Florida to visit Disney World. My husband and I had gone there on a second leg of our honeymoon and then had visited again when he had just started graduate school, but after a four-year absence, I was yearning to get back to one of my favorite fantasy places. I figured this trip was a good time to go because I was ready for another pass at Disney, and even though the children would probably not fully appreciate and remember it, at least they were small enough that I didn't have to pay for them yet. I could write pages about my fondness of Disney and the magic that seems to linger in the air like so much Tinkerbell dust, but I will simply touch on one aspect of the place that held my interest from my first visit at age thirteen.

Epcot Center seemed quite futuristic at its first opening, but now after twenty years the whole fifteen acres just seems ho-hum contemporary; frankly, it's dated, and it's hard to get excited by souped-up personal computers, which everyone has at home now. So aside from the grouping of foreign countries in miniature — which will always interest me because they're the next best thing to traveling the globe, which I can't afford yet — Epcot has little to excite me anymore as a jaded, tech-savvy adult. But one exhibit I loved as a child and enjoyed again with my own little girls was one that will never go out of style, will never be outdated or antique like rotary phones or pre-Windows computers.

The topic? A very simple idea, really — Imagination. One feature is the standard ride on a large conveyor-belt with seats, and it introduces the visitors to some standard Disney-fied whimsical characters. The main character was named Figment, for "figment of your imagination." Figment captured my thirteen-year-old imagination and still drifts through my adult mind. I bought myself a stuffed animal, of course, at the end of the ride, *de rigeur* for a tourist my age, and a friend brought me a keychain featuring Figment a short while later after her trip to the same locale. I still have the animal, which sits among my daughter's and my collection in her room, and the scratched, dulled clear plastic keychain ornament is all that adorns my set of keys even now, all these years later.

The pink-and-purple dragon-like character is just a mascot for the flights of fancy on which I remember embarking daily as a child and on which I am still a flier, but just not enough to accrue too many frequent-flier miles. Figment — and the theme song which accompanied the ride, "a dream can be a dream come true ..." — are reminders to me of the cherished dreams I had as a youngster and that I don't have to grow out of as an adult. These flights of fancy are free and open up whole new worlds of possibility.

My mother remarked often about how creative and imaginative I was when I was growing up. She was fascinated by the stories I could tell and the ideas that came into my head. I am seeing this now with my own daughter, in a sort of cosmic maternal *déjà vu* experience. The scenes my mother experienced with me are playing out again twenty-five years later.

One of Brianna's creative skills now is spinning elaborate, complete scenarios from one sentence or picture in a book. When we read, sometimes we pause in between sentences or pages for a good long while so she can explain to me the *real* story. If I'm smart, I listen carefully and enjoy the moment, trying to see where she is getting her material, and trying to jump into her bright, busy, detailed world. If not, if I'm tired or impatient or ready to move on, I either tune out for a moment and hear nothing she says or I try to quell her and get her to cease and desist the whole elaborate story gig.

I think back on all the scenes that were in my head when I was growing up, some raw material coming from the many books I read, and some spun purely from my own imagination. I wrote and illustrated stories and "books" made from typing paper and staples. My mom kept several, which are enshrined in my childhood scrapbook. They're simple affairs, written in smudged pencil or black ballpoint ink, with immature illustrations, but they remind me even now that I had an entire world of my own in my head, and the books were simply repositories of the stuff that exploded out from that world onto paper.

In light of this hobby I engaged in so frequently as a youth, it seems odd to me now that I never imagined writing a book until just a few years ago. I never even was interested in writing as a career choice until my senior year in high school, when my all-wise mother suggested I take journalism. My junior-year honors history teacher was going to be teaching the journalism class my senior year, and since I had enjoyed her class and learned a great deal from her the year before, my mom told me I might as well give her class a shot. At that stage of my life, I didn't consider myself a writer, but Mom did. Perhaps she remembered all of those paper books.

Luckily, in spite of being a teenager, I didn't reject Mom's suggestion out of hand, but I decided the idea had merit and enrolled in the class, which turned out not only to be a whole lot of fun my senior year but which also convinced me to drop my planned chemistry major and go for a journalism degree in college. And here I am, writing this book now.

I'm writing about my daughter's bursts of creativity that come so naturally to her in hopes that it will remind me of my own days of unmitigated flights of fancy and creation. I mentioned already my hobby of writing stories and books when I was younger, but I also indulged in a number of other interests. I dabbled in architecture: I would regularly pull out large pieces of paper, pencils and rulers and go to work for several hours on designing elaborate, to-scale house plans, complete with tiny sketches of furniture. Another favorite pastime was to set up a mail system in my house, taping together paper mailboxes and posting them on each bedroom door, then delivering mail to each box, an original paper stamp (drawn by *moi*) affixed to each envelope. I even made family newspapers and delivered those to the boxes too. I was my own publisher and delivery system in one. As I think back on those newspapers, I find it doubly fascinating that I didn't recognize my inherent early interest in publishing. Not a writer or a journalist, indeed! I can't believe I wouldn't have pursued it without my mom's intervention. (Yeah, yeah, Mom, thanks to you.)

Those early forays into different hobbies provided me opportunities to explore what interested me, and obviously, some of those trial careers turned into what I have done professionally as an adult. But imagination isn't just a means to an end, a way to find the right path to making money, being successful and becoming entrenched in the "real world;" it's really more about exploring oneself and taking joy in all the possibilities that lie within and without. Watching Brianna's forays into her own abundant, joyous, and all-encompassing creativity has sparked not only pleasant reminders of the same joy and color that expanded and lit up my life as a child; it has brought more richness and color into my black-and-white, fiscally-driven and practical life today. Imagination truly is making a dream come true, just like my little pal Figment promised me.

While creativity often is associated with the notion of sending out free-floating, swirling ideas that are bigger than life yet still able to soar in the mists of the mind, it still can involve quite a bit of real work, practice, and trial and error. And practicing something to achieve mastery or greatness or just satisfaction necessarily involves the ability to let go of self-consciousness and fear of failure. These qualities are not readily found in adults (I'm speaking for myself here, at least), but I've seen that ability to let go and just get immersed in the task at hand in my daughter as she's exercised her imagination.

For instance, one afternoon I was taking a much-needed bath (as in, I was extremely sweaty and smelly after a hard workout, so I needed to get clean, but more importantly, I was in need of a brief period of relaxation and miraculously was able to steal a few minutes to rest quietly in my tub of warm, bubbly water). I had accomplished this feat by leaving Brianna to watch a new (and free!) acquisition to our burgeoning library of animated videos. (Yes, it's video babysitting, but it is effective and vital at times.)

As I lay in my pseudo-private, quiet haven, I could hear one of the songs from this musical movie begin, the notes and words wafting in past the partially-closed door.

I heard the characters singing the words of the song and the accompaniment; I also heard my daughter attempting to sing. She was humming and throwing in a word here and there, some right on cue, but most a split-second behind what the characters were singing. So if the song went something like this: "Candy is terrific, it really floats my boat," according to the video, Brianna was doing this: "Hm candy hm da da da, da dada floats da da hm BOAT!" I felt sure that next time she heard the song she would get this far: "Candy hm terrific, da da floats MY BOAT!" And the next would be just about perfect. Soon after, every time she heard the song, she would be in the running for a Grammy for most accurate and enthusiastic performance of an annoying preschool song destined to stick in the heads of nearby parents.

I grinned to myself, realizing that it was another of those special moments in which I was observing my daughter in the process of learning. And as she was learning, she gave no thought to how she must sound or look to outsiders. She was completely focused on learning, and eventually on getting it right.

In ten years, she will have forgotten this method and will have switched over to the method of learning in secret, that which youth and adults use, and which isn't nearly as effective. We older people enjoy the concept of learning, as in acquiring new knowledge or skills, but don't enjoy as much the process of learning, which involves practice. The practice is tedious, for one thing, and for another, it makes us look silly or stupid. What would be ideal is if we could be completely ignorant or unskilled one day, then after finding we have a desire to learn the new skill, we could own it immediately, as if we could just purchase a CD-ROM off Amazon.com and download it directly into the proper area of our brains.

One particular example of the real, and difficult, way of learning comes to mind — shared by a teacher, of course. I remember my junior high school band instructor quite clearly. He was a very strong personality, with a quick and strong temper and a great deal of talent and charisma. He had one of the best bands in the area, probably because of his incredible knowledge, drive and motivational skills. (One very memorable one: sometimes he threw chairs when practice wasn't going well.) And classes were never boring, not just because of flying chairs or podiums: this teacher — notice I name no names here — was very entertaining and funny, though occasionally I became the object of his teasing. Having just moved to the South from Pennsylvania, my Northern accent, one which I felt was the proper and normal way of speaking, made me stick out like a, well, a Yankee in Mississippi. ("Niiiine??" I remember him parroting, exaggerated and mocking, clearly pointing out the already obvious and huge difference between my pronunciation of an often-used number and the almost unrecognizable Southern dialectical "nahn").

On a more positive note and most importantly, my band teacher would command each of us, "If you're going to make a mistake, do it loudly." He didn't want us practicing hesitantly and quietly, so as to hide a mistake if we made one. He wanted us to boldly and confidently practice our notes; if we made a mistake, it would be obvious to everyone, but at least we would be getting the most out of our practice sessions. We wouldn't be pussyfooting our way through our most valuable learn-to-get-it-right time, depriving ourselves of learning to play properly.

I don't believe I ever followed this advice. I was too embarrassed, too self-conscious about letting other people know I wasn't perfect. I still am. Here lies one of my greatest weaknesses. Recently, I was asked to sing at a family member's wedding reception. I am not a professional; I have never had voice lessons, and I rarely sing. Nonetheless, I have a reasonably pleasant voice, enjoy music and have some training in other musical expressions (remember band?). So I agreed, somewhat reluctantly, to take on this task.

I had only a few weeks to prepare myself, for a variety of reasons unnecessary to mention here. I sang alone, in the car. Even my husband heard me sing the piece only a few times before the day of the wedding. I stressed and fretted about how bad I was going to sound. I let only myself hear, and that only because it was impossible to produce notes from my mouth without my close-by ears overhearing the performance. I hoped by not hearing myself too much I could forget that I didn't like what I did hear, and I hoped that my music somehow would never be heard by anyone else.

That little delusion would have to change by performance day. The night before the wedding, my husband's family and I were setting up and decorating the reception hall. The karaoke machine was primed with its tapes of accompaniment for those of us who planned to sing. The other two singers practiced over and over, confidently and in full earshot of those who were helping to set up. I knew I needed practice, but I dreaded being judged as a bad singer. Finally, I allowed myself to sing quietly, not with the microphone. I sang a few times that way and then managed to force myself to sing into the microphone, so all could hear. Then I found that wasn't too bad, so I practiced it as it would sound the next day.

I did alright; I sounded fine during my real performance. I still wouldn't say it was the best performance of that particular song or even my best performance of any song. But I seem to have pleased those who heard it and those who asked me to sing in the first place. I just think now that if I hadn't been so afraid for others to hear me while I was practicing to get it right, I would have sounded better on performance day. But I was too fearful, nervous that I would sound bad to the few bystanders. I didn't want to be embarrassed.

But that's what practice and learning is about: it's the process of getting something right. It doesn't happen immediately. My daughter knows this and isn't afraid to sound bad in the practicing stage. She has an understanding of the process. I'm hoping that some day she'll also understand that not just skills but all of life is a learning process. I'm figuring that out myself, and trying to cut myself some slack as I slowly learn the biggest skills of all: how to be a mom and how to just be me. Luckily, I have some good help, mentors and cheering sections, primarily involving the same people: my mom and my daughters.

Life and the world around us provide an endless stream of "home-school" subjects, I've noticed. Many of these subjects seem to be universally attractive to kids. For instance, Brianna alerts me to the presence of ants whenever she gets wind of one of them being close by. After sounding the alarm that we have one or more little workers, she stares intently at the ant and keeps me abreast of its every move, as if the ant is the subject of a Discovery Channel docu-drama and she is the intelligent and suave narrator. The ant either goes about its business as if nothing is happening and it has not suddenly been thrust into the spotlight or stops and wonders in its tiny little brain what in the world is going on. "Why," it thinks, "am I the focus of such intent scrutiny? I'm just walking around, carrying bits of dust from my mound to inside this huge wooden structure. Even my wife doesn't think this is too interesting, and my kids never tag along for take-your-pupa-to-work day. I think I'll just keep walking."

However uninterested his kids may be, my kid is fascinated. She can stare and stare and then comment. Frankly, I am just as uninterested. I've got too many other things to do than look at the lowly creature who sometimes infests my home if I leave food out (which, by the way, is easy to do with kids and their way of absent-mindedly leaving crackers and cups of milk in odd places). Apparently, however, once upon a time, I was just as fascinated as Brianna is now. This is not a fact that springs from my memory, but from my mother's. She has told me numerous times since I've been an adult how much she enjoyed watching me scrutinize the world around me, particularly when I analyzed ants. She thought it was amazing that I could stop in the middle of a walk with her, squat down, and center my attention on a string of ants. She says I could sit there for hours. Or at least half an hour. She really delighted in watching the little me, already close to the ground, crouch down and learn about the ant world by close, scientific observation.

Perhaps my mother was wiser than I. I don't take the time as often to sit and savor the spectacle of my daughter as she learns (or practices for her future occupation of documentary film maker). But when I do, I enjoy it. She hasn't become bored yet with the ubiquitous little creatures populating our world. She hasn't reached the point where she thinks she knows it all about her environment. Every new discovery is an adventure.

Bubbles are another wonderful science project. Kids love 'em. A simple but perfect sphere, translucent and shimmering in the sunlight, created by blowing air into a wand dipped in soapy water, transfixes the attention of children and excites their imaginations incredibly. My daughter can leap around for a good hour or more, blowing until her round, pink little cheeks are probably sore and tuckered out from all that puckering, yelling and squealing delightedly. She watches the bubbles form, carefully trying to make them larger and grander. She tries to blow them up toward the sky, waving around. She bursts them, analyzing them as they transform from a large sphere to a tiny dot of dew, accompanied by a tiny popping sound. She loves the process of making them and deflating them, and all the fun in between. I figure she's learning a little bit about nature — physics, chemistry, what-have-you.

And then there's zoology — the endless array of animals available for observation, like bunnies, squirrels, birds. Brianna tries continually to approach birds and squirrels who frequent our yard. She has yet to run towards one who is inclined to stay put and allow the gigantic stranger charging full-speed at it to interrupt its daily, peaceful routine. Her yelling and squealing probably don't help. But she keeps trying. Perhaps I should make her some peanut-butter sandwiches — that worked for me when I was her age, I hear. My mother managed to help me tame some backyard squirrels when I was little; they seemed to like homemade whole-wheat peanut-butter sandwiches so much that they came up to the back door and begged for us to hand over the tiny squares to them. I loved it, and now we have permanent proof in the form of pictures of a squirrel waiting on the step for that sandwich.

Paying attention to the world around us and its milieu of living creatures is entertaining and intriguing: truly an adventure. When Brianna stops to look at the ants or the squirrels or birds, I must stop and gaze too. As I watch a squirrel hopping on light feet from my lawn into a nearby tree, I feel more connected to the earth on which we live, more a part of it all. I get caught up in the magic of the little lives led by these creatures so different from me. I feel more connected to the child in me who used to feed sandwiches to those pesky squirrels, and to the pert and petite brunette mother who assembled them. And last, but not least, I am sharing this grand adventure, along with all its delight and excitement, with the most magical creature I know — my daughter.

Of course, I couldn't and can't spend all my time outside; as a child, I did plenty of exploring indoors, as does my daughter now. Most of that creative time is spent in nooks and crannies, boxes and stacks of paper, despite the billions of dollars spent each year by advertisers hawking gadgets in between cartoons.

Sure, kids can't help but be drawn to the expensive, flashy, technology-driven latest "it" toys: the Tickle Me Elmos, the morphing action heroes, the Barbies and Barneys that interact with computer software. This is the kind of stuff that inspires "I've really been good this year" letters to Santa and puppy-dog-faced personal pleas to parents across the world come Christmastime. Box-office hits have been made about how parents feel crushed by the pressure to get the coolest new fad-toys for their deprived little urchins each year.

But parents around the globe have also witnessed year after year how those fancy toys get left in a heap in a dark corner nanoseconds after the thrill of the new bell or whistle wears off. A very popular animated movie told the tale about a fancy new toy replacing the old for a while, and what kind of inter-toy struggles ensued there.

After it's all said and done, the old standards tend to last the longest and get played with the most, particularly after the new toys have worn out their flashy but brief welcome. Legos, Lincoln Logs, Tinkertoys, wooden blocks — most have been around for years and have been updated slightly by toy companies to ensure their staying power in an ever-more-hungry-for-technology world. But they are essentially the same and always fun to play with.

Why? Why in the world do kids always go back to the basic toys, which aren't much to speak of in terms of razzle-dazzle? Because instead of coming completely assembled as one toy, they are raw materials for dozens, even hundreds, of toys, given a little time and imagination. The children can assemble them into whatever preposterous creation they can dream up. The imagined toy is fun to play with once created, but even better, the journey is the most fun part — simply fashioning dreams into reality.

My daughter has reminded me that not only the basic toys are fun, but basic household items are useful as raw materials as well. She can dive into the pots and pans, newspapers, old tools, even fine china (not one of my favorites for raw material) to create something fun. She stacks cans of food or old, beat-up boxes or Tupperware in order of color or size; she puts them on top of each other, inside each other, whatever she can imagine to create something that exists in reality or only in her mind. And I don't have to spend a dime (unless she breaks that china!) for her to have her fun. She's not pleading piteously for a new toy; she's using what she already has.

I remember doing that myself. As I watch her work intently on creating unique toys for herself, which will end up being recycled the next day as a new item, I remember building my own fantasies as a child and young person, as I did with my writing and illustration, my post-office game, and my architecture. My mom didn't have to buy much for me to enjoy these flights of fantasy.

As I grew older and went off to college, I still had to put my creativity to work to make things for myself. I didn't have much spending money during my school days, so my apartment wasn't decorated in style, with framed pictures on the walls or nice slipcovers for the brown plaid furniture or even matching bed-in-a-bag sets. My roommates and I made do with the basics we already had and were able to scrounge from relatives, who were generally perfectly happy to pawn off beat-up old pans and skillets and mismatched spatulas, plates, and "silverware" on us. We found old art prints and sticky-tacked them to the walls; we rearranged the fourthhand, pressed-board coffee and end tables, couch and chairs until they seemed almost unique to our apartment and not carbon copies of every single other unit in our building. I made the half of my bedroom my own with snapshots, notes from guys, posters, and event stubs tacked onto the wall next to my bed and desk. Three-dollar red and yellow plastic crates served for storage space for clothes and junk I couldn't part with. "Better Dorm Rooms and Gardens" it was not but it was personal, my first "on-my-own" space and quite homey.

It didn't change too much after I graduated and got married. My husband went to graduate school for two years shortly after our wedding, so as "poor married students," we still didn't have a lot to speak of. My red and yellow college crates stacked up and held most of my sweaters and pants, no different than a few years before, and even more cheap plastic shelving worked fine for all of my precious photo albums and journals. Many of our wedding gifts were very nice and made us feel rich compared to college (unfortunately, we lacked a china

cabinet in which to store all those chip-and-dip trays and crys-
tal bowls), but we are much more well equipped now that my
husband is out of school and gainfully employed. It's been
absolutely delightful being able to buy some real furniture for
our bedroom and make our girls' bedroom look like a planned
nursery rather than a mismatched jumble of donated and
cheaply acquired items. However, occasionally I still miss the
days I was forced to be more creative. It's just too easy to be
able to go out and purchase something that's "needed." That's
probably been why I took up sewing recently, so I could make
something that was uniquely my own, with or even without a
pattern, just with some fabric and my imagination. It's been
fun, creating something useful and beautiful that's an extension of myself. Hm. I could say the same about Brianna.

Along the lines of indoor activities, I remember building
forts all the time. One of my favorite things to do was to
arrange the dining or living room chairs into a square or circle
and drape them with a blanket or sheet. The setup immediately would be transformed into a cozy, private cottage of my
own. If I became really ambitious, I would make several rooms
with more chairs and sheets — a whole mansion. My mother
was kind enough to indulge me with this for most of a day, not
requiring me to clean up and dismantle my house until it was
time to eat dinner. It was always a bit of a letdown to take it
all apart. Every piece of my glorious structure had to go back
to its ordained usage and the imagined dream home would be
gone in a poof, like Cinderella and her beautiful coach at mid-
night. Pumpkins all.

Now my dreams of beautiful homes revolve around clippings from *Better Homes and Gardens*, collected practical ideas for renovating or redecorating my existing home or trading up for a nicer or bigger home. But it all comes down to the fact that they are practical and real and I am an adult now, paying for a real house. My daughter is now the one imagining from scratch, creating dreams and visions that cost no money and require no clippings. What she imagines right now is a mystery to me because she doesn't tell me much of what's in her head. All I get are peeks into the windows of her mind when she pulls up a shade.

Last week when I was trying to put Brianna to bed was one of these window-opening occasions. She took a detour from the usual routine of brushing teeth, reading, and so on, the motions of which I walk through carefully but eagerly until I can quietly leave her room and enjoy peace and quiet for a few minutes before my own exhausted head crashes onto my pillow. After we brushed her teeth and before we attacked the chosen stack of books, she got in her bed, with me joining her, and she lifted the sheets high up and put them over our heads so we were in a little wonderland of our own. Instantly we were not just in her room, with deceptive old Mommy trying to trick the energetic little girl into sleeping. We were in a special world where we could both be little girls and giggle together for a few minutes. It was magical for me; I felt for a moment that we were child comrades, cohorts having fun together and imagining together.

I was taken back to those times of building my sheet houses and sitting inside them, imagining the soft-walled homes were huge, intricate palaces. I remember the solitude and the freedom to feel I was whatever I wanted to be inside. I was free to go anywhere and be anyone. I could build as much as I wanted to, given enough chairs and sheets. All it took was the power of imagination. That ability to let go of the limits of reality is much easier for children; as we turn into adults, we find ourselves locked into the small concrete box of hard, cold reality and unable to soar free in our minds. Our worlds may truly be limited in some fashion by the facts of reality, but our minds and our dreams don't have those constraints. We just come to imagine they do.

Brianna's fort that evening consisted of billowing a sheet over our heads. Sheets formed the walls and ceilings of my pretend houses, where I dreamed big. Her act of pumping the sheet and letting it form a mushroomy cloud over and around us also took me back to a few isolated days in elementary school that allowed me to imagine myself being somewhere new and exotic.

One day in second or third grade was "Yellow Submarine" day at school. Our teachers got hold of a balloony plastic submarine, which our entire class inflated and squeezed into en masse. The teachers played the famous Beatles record (which I'd never heard because my parents were a little old to be part of that Fab Four generation) and we sat inside and discussed what it would be like to be underwater. I can't recall anything else or what it was we were *supposed* to learn from that day — aquatic life? marine biology? — I just remember the sensation of being inside a vessel of imagination.

The other event in elementary school was a rare activity in gym class, that of playing with a parachute. It was my favorite activity, one that unfortunately didn't occur nearly as often as kickball or dodgeball (which I heartily disliked). Our gym class gathered around the diameter of a circle of parachute material, large enough for twenty or thirty of us to grab with two hands with a space of a person between each of us, and then on a count, we yanked the parachute quickly down and then high up in the air and on the last step, down on the floor behind us, so we all ended up sitting in a circle inside the parachute that had transformed into a kind of temporary Biosphere. It was nifty. I was in a fort with a bunch of other kids, in a breezy, intimate space that was far away from the sterile old gymnasium of beat-up wooden floors and rickety bleachers. I loved being in that alternate world and sharing it with my classmates. I hated for the class period to end, and in my memory, we only got to enjoy that little dream world a few times in a year or two. The rest of the time was dreaded hours of that sadistic sport called dodgeball and rope-climbing.

So now I'm a grown-up, years removed from those dreamy bouts of shared imagination, but Brianna has the power to jolt me out of my world of concrete reality and lure me down a hole like the rabbit does to Alice in Wonderland. All she has to do to make me shrink or grow large, borrowing from Lewis Carroll, is to pull a pink sheet over my head and join me in a fort. It's so easy for her.

I enjoyed the few moments we shared, out of time as two happy little girls able to do and be whatever we wanted. But then the spell was broken, my desire for sleep overcoming the fun little world. I leapt out of the hole and zoomed right back to my universe of hard, cold reality. But I'd like to go back. I hope she wants to let me in again.

PART V
FULL CIRCLE

CHAPTER 13
JUST LIKE MOM

I like old movies. I particularly like old musicals, the classic sound-staged films in which every other word is sung and danced. As corny as they are, musicals are pure fun and participatory entertainment. It's impossible to hear "Seventy-six Trombones" from *The Music Man* without wanting to get up and march around the room imitating the deep bleats of the horns or to watch *Oklahoma* without joining right in on the crescendo of "oooooOOOOHHHHHK!-la-homa" and feeling the wind sweeping around the plain of the living room. My personal favorite is the "I'm Just a Girl Who Cain't Say No" song; it's innocent yet not and goofily funny. I sing along every time and laugh, even though none of the punch lines are surprises to me anymore.

Perhaps I enjoy musicals so much because my life has seemed like a musical. My growing-up years and now my married years have a soundtrack. My daughter has either been born with the innate ability to make a song out of everything or she has picked it up from everyone else in the family. She feels comfortable belting out a song, no matter what kind of song, anytime. The song can be one she's learned along the way, or one she's making up as she goes along. Either way, she fits right in.

My mom used popular songs to punctuate her spoken words. One I remember most was "Please Release Me," a Conway Twitty or some other country song. She would grab us and hold us tight and squeeze and hug, while we half-protested to be set free from her grasp. I really don't know why we did this; it just somehow evolved as a tradition of sorts. Mom hugged and squeezed, and when we pleaded "let me go!" she launched into "Pleeee-ase release me, let me go" and would laugh and let us free. The problem now is that I have no idea how the rest of the song goes. More lyrics do exist, but they are unknown to us because only the first few words were apropos to our little game.

Mom could pull songs from her memory for use in these kinds of situations, and she could also create her own. She would make up rambling, ridiculous tunes to accompany whatever we were doing. Usually, it was as an incentive to just get something done, such as cleaning or getting ready for bed. The tunes and the un-rhyming, extemporaneous prose were gone the next day, but they served their purpose in the interim: we were forced to obey her wishes just to get her to stop singing! All three of us kids complained loudly that Mom just couldn't carry a tune, and she tried to assure us that she really could sing. Recently, she informed me with a note of triumph in her voice that she did in fact SING in some productions in high school, not just participate in speaking roles. I had to hand it to her that at least one time in her life she must have been able to carry a tune; I'm still not going to retroactively modify my childhood opinion drastically.

I find myself making up songs now too. One night a few weeks ago, I decided a little distraction was needed to lure Brianna away from other activities and get her interested in brushing her teeth. So I used the melody of a rock song and crooned loudly, dancing a goofy dance along with it, "Brush, brush, brush your teeth — everybody brush your teeth" over and over until Brianna thought it was funny enough she wanted to join in. It worked — she became focused on cleaning her teeth, but the drawback was she wanted to sing for a while ABOUT brushing before she decided to get down to the nitty-gritty and do it.

My husband is a big influence in this arena, too. In fact, he may be more adept than I. He has a song for everything. He has a fantastic memory for song lyrics, movie lines, and old TV commercials, so any innocently-spoken phrase can set him off into quoting from these sources. Some are familiar to me and some obscure; either way, he cracks me up. After eight years of marriage, I am still amazed at his ability to remember phrases he sometimes only heard once. It makes me laugh and always lightens the mood. He also makes up his own songs occasionally, too, when he seems unable to pull an appropriate lyric out of his vast memorized collection. So our house is full of goofy songs, injunctions to get things done.

Being creative, attaching established or made-up songs to everyday mundane events, makes life a little lighter. We laugh a little more, we smile and chuckle. There's more incentive to go ahead and brush the teeth or get the lawn mown if we laugh a little or go into the chore with a song in our head and heart. The melodies trail behind, even after the music is over; the air seems to be carrying bits and pieces of notes as we walk through it and breathe it in. Those notes lift me up and make me happier and cheerier, and most importantly remind me of the loved ones who created them. Even though I don't remember now the particular songs or lyrics that my mother sang when I was growing up, I remember the feelings. I will remember forever the connections, the laughter, the silliness, the crazy affection I feel now as my husband and my daughter sing me their goofy ditties. Here's hoping our corny musicals live forever in my daughter's memory too.

Around the time I brought a new baby home to join the family, my tiny two-year-old daughter started using a phrase, accompanied by specific gestures, that was very funny and entertaining — and eerily familiar. This pint-size authority figure would put one hand on her hip, the other hand poking out with index finger pointing dramatically, and say in a serious, pay-attention tone of voice: "I'll be right back." As in, "don't move a muscle while I'm gone!" My mother, who was here to help me with the new baby, and I would just laugh and talk about how cute and grown-up it was. After a few days of the visit, and close observation, my mom figured out the origin of this hilarious affectation; she pointed out that I was doing the same thing. Every time I left the room to change a diaper or grab another wipe or burp cloth, I would tell my older daughter, "I'll be right back." Same tone of voice, same words, same everything.

Since then the list of phrases and gestures has grown to lines such as "You're being disobedient. Go to time-out" (to which my daughter sometimes adds her own twist of "Cry!" in an imperious tone of voice); "Eat your ice cream at the table" and "Sit down. Don't play with my food?" All are just parrotings of what I have said at one time or another and continue to tell her on an as-needed basis. Not only does she nail the actual phrase, but she mimics completely accurately the tone of voice, the facial expressions, and the accompanying gestures.

This is all entertaining, of course, until I find that she's repeating something that wasn't very nice (like a stray expletive) or really appropriate for a small girl to say. What I've said is coming back to haunt me, and I do have to watch very carefully what I say around her now.

I haven't just taught her what to say; I've taught her what to do. This, as with the phrases, can be really entertaining or embarrassing because she may be imitating something that I shouldn't be doing in the first place, or something that I wouldn't do in front of a crowd of strangers. My husband finds it particularly amusing when Brianna mimics breast-feeding her baby doll. She sees me nurse her baby sister, so naturally she figures that's how she'll feed her dolly. She holds the doll, lifts up her shirt, and cradles the doll to her chest, murmuring encouraging words such as "There you go" or "Eat up." She also tells us to be quiet, when "her baby" is sleeping.

She copies how I eat, how I brush my teeth, how I clean or cook. She irons or does laundry (and now doesn't have to pretend as much because her grandma bought her a toy laundry set). She wants to vacuum and stir cake batter or eggs (thank goodness she hasn't tried what I did at her age — stirring eggs into the carpet with a wooden spoon while my mom stirred eggs, milk, yeast, and flour for bread dough). She watches me exercise to my aerobics videos and starts doing leg lifts and ab crunches right along with me. I've got a "mini-me" running around, who, thanks to the powerful genes of my husband, doesn't seem to be exhibiting any of my physical characteristics at all.

All of these imitations are of behaviors or phrases that I don't intentionally try to teach her. She just picks them up, watching my every move. I do intend to teach her how to read, how to crack an egg and pour it into a pan, how to make her bed, how to pronounce new words. She does well with those things I'm trying to get her to learn, but she picks up just as easily (or more so) those things she watches me do day in and day out and which I'm not actively teaching her.

I grew up learning from my mom how to cook and do other household tasks. She made homemade bread, so I made bread too (though carefully supervised). She turned out three or four loaves at a time, a hefty amount of sticky dough. As she worked, she would give each of my siblings and me a cereal bowl of our own with tiny amounts of the same ingredients she was using. We stirred, we kneaded, we shaped into little loaves, we waited as they rose and baked. Today I bake bread myself, sometimes in big batches like my mom made. I often give some of the loaves away. People ask how I came to learn how to make such good bread, all by myself, in my own kitchen (no mix, no breadmaker, no devices whatsoever but elbow grease and time). Seems pretty simple to me, but from what I can tell, it seems to be a fading art.

Mom also made cakes and cookies from scratch. I enjoyed decorating cakes so much that Mom let me make cakes for birthdays all by myself. I became quite skilled at making cakes look almost professional; I made a baseball out of a round cake for my brother one year, and I piped an iced Garfield on a cake for my sister. Looking back, I still am amazed that I was able, at age twelve or thirteen, to create a recognizable comic-strip character out of very dark frosting, squeezed out of a pastry bag. I was afraid I had lost that talent but found that I was just able to create a favorite cartoon character on a cake for my younger daughter's latest birthday.

The clincher in all this fun expression of creativity with the mediums of butter and powdered sugar was that it usually took me half an hour to make enough frosting to decorate a cake. I could whip up the cake in no time but would dread the painstaking middle step of that thirty-minute work on the frosting; it was such a hassle trying to get the perfect consistency, adding a tiny bit of milk, then a bit more powdered sugar, then a half-teaspoon more of milk, then more powdered sugar. I wanted Mom to do it for me. But she refused – coldheartedly so, I thought. She told me that if I wanted to decorate, I'd have to learn to make the frosting myself, even if it did take me the time I could have spent reading half a book. But today, thanks to years of wisely enforced practice, I can whip up a batch of frosting in two minutes flat, without a second thought, just like Mom did so effortlessly years ago. I also get enthusiastic compliments about my homemade, preservative-free frosting.

Sweets aren't the only items I learned to make in the kitchen — healthier fare like breakfasts and main dishes became part of my repertoire. I liked a certain chicken dish called tetrazinni. My mom did it for a while, and I'd watch and help. Then, after I'd watched her numerous times, she told me to take over. I remember one day making tetrazinni all by myself. I think I started preparations for dinner at three o'clock in the afternoon. I ended up working steadily all the way up until dinnertime. Today, well, you get the picture. I don't have to start quite so early (and I admit that sometimes now I take shortcuts and use canned chicken or leftover holiday turkey – but that's my prerogative now that I've mastered the fundamentals).

My two siblings were also guided to make their own fare. My little brother liked pancakes so much he seemed to want them every day for breakfast. So Mom decided it was time for him to learn how to make them himself. After a little while, he didn't even need a recipe. The vertically-challenged chef expertly pulled up a chair, took the ingredients out of the cupboard, mixed them together, and had pancakes on the table in short order.

Perhaps I've focused on food to illustrate Mom's teaching method because I am so fond of eating, but that doesn't mean the only thing my mom taught me was cooking. She taught me how to make my bed, how to clean the bathroom, how to vacuum, even dust. (That last one was never my favorite, so even though I knew what to do, it was always the last chore on my list to get done on any given Saturday morning. Even today I probably still only dust once a month when the layers covering my furniture obscure its natural color, but I am sure to bring out the dust rag for those special occasions when Mom, the inspector general, visits.)

She taught me how to read, how to write, how to draw. She taught me to follow my dreams, to think big, and to believe in myself. I hope that I can pass all these legacies on to my daughter, in addition to my pet phrases of "I'll be right back" and "You're in time out!"

So now when I have a question or want to learn something new, I still usually go to my mom. It's so much more effective than learning from some degreed expert's class or book, and it's much more fun. And I get to spend time with someone I love and respect a great deal. I did it growing up, and my daughter is smart enough to be doing it now for herself. It seems to be working well for her.

The moment my second daughter was born, and even before, people were asking me how Brianna was doing with it.

How was she adjusting to having another child in the house: was she feeling displaced, was she excited about having a smaller person around, was she angry about having attention drawn away from herself, was she happy or confused?

At first, she seemed mainly curious about the tiny new addition to the family, and she seemed intent on testing her out. What was this person able to do? Did she mind being hit? Yes, for a few weeks Brianna would calmly and dispassionately thump Marissa in the stomach. She didn't seem angry, frustrated or jealous; I really have no idea why she would hit her in this manner, though I can speculate that she was trying to get a reaction or interaction or that she wanted to find out what she could get away with. She found out quickly that although the baby didn't usually react loudly to her thumping, Mom and Dad sure would.

Mostly, however, after that phase passed, and she was seemingly adjusted to having a little sister, queries from acquaintances or strangers moved along the lines of "Is Brianna a good big sister?" or "Is Brianna her mommy's little helper?" I laughed at this line of questioning because I didn't feel like my two-year-old was much use in the "helping" department. After all, she couldn't change a diaper, nurse the baby, or put her to sleep (or get up with her in the middle of the night), so I was out of luck for a while with my big needs.

As time has moved on, with Marissa reaching the year marker and Brianna maturing from a toddler into a young girl, I've changed my tune. Brianna is a big helper, in her own way, within her capabilities. I just had to learn to be creative with small things that would allow her to contribute and then give her the opportunities to carry out those small responsibilities.

One of the first, easiest things I could ask Brianna to do was to fetch a clean diaper and wipes or to throw away a dirty diaper of Marissa's. I would tell her, "It would really help me if you could get a diaper, Brianna." She'd eagerly run off to their bedroom and return quickly with the right size diaper, and I would thank her and tell her that was a big help and made things easier for Mommy. She seemed pleased to contribute.

Next, as Marissa grew a little older and began adding pureed baby food to her menu, Brianna became very interested in feeding her herself. As I got out all the mealtime paraphernalia for baby — bib, jars of food, spoon, napkins, wet cloths, and so on — big sister would be drawn to the spectacle as surely as if Barney himself had suddenly appeared in her dining room. Her body would almost magnetically attach itself to the scene of the meal, and she would plead for a chance to take charge of the spoon, dip it into the jars of food and guide it to her sister's open baby-bird mouth. I indulged her desire to get involved by allowing her to take turns with me as she learned to navigate gloppy food the twelve inches or so from jar to messy, eager mouth. Marissa became impatient sometimes, so every so often I would take over briefly from Brianna and satiate baby with a few quick, expertly guided spoonfuls. Then Brianna was able to do a few spoonfuls herself, and she even learned to mix the vegetables with the fruit as I did because Marissa was a little picky. Even now, Brianna loves to participate in mealtime. Sure, I could do it faster and just get it done, but as I learn my lessons in patience, my older daughter gets to learn her lessons in doing her part.

As she has gotten older, she has also graduated to higher levels of cleaning up. First, all she could really do was put away her own toys. Lately, though, she has taken new interest in the cleaning chores I do around the house. As I have made my bed and hers, she has stepped up to the other side and chirped,

"Can I help?" I guide her through the motions of pulling up the sheets, then the quilt, and then putting the pillows on and folding the quilt over the pillows. Her enthusiasm for this banal daily ritual has been invigorating. She's so excited to do something like Mommy does.

This is also true with cooking and baking and scrubbing the sink or bathtub. The last few times I've attacked the bathtub, Brianna has even been drawn away from favorite videos to join me on the floor of the bathroom. Oh sure, I can see the appeal of this bucolic domestic scene: here's Mommy, leaning precariously over the side of the hard, slippery porcelain tub, working up a sweat with some Comet and a scrub brush. Hard work versus leisure. Tough choice. But Brianna, amazingly, has wanted to get in on the action. I hand her the toothbrush, and I continue my circular motions with the larger brush, and together we get the tub and the fixtures looking bright, shiny, and dirt-free. After we rinse out the gritty residue, we are free to stand proudly together next to the gleaming tub and admire our work.

As much as I work up a sweat on this weekly chore, I've always felt a sense of accomplishment afterward. I like the sense of comparing the before and after shots in my head, and the satisfaction that my elbow grease made such a glistening difference. I've had this feeling ever since I was a small child, that a clean bathroom is something to feel proud of, and now Brianna is joining me in that small victory. No wonder she doesn't mind the break from *Cinderella* — on the screen, she sees Cinderella sloshing water and soapsuds around the entryway floor, but in her own bathroom, she can sling around real water and suds in person with Mom.

As Brianna and I bond in our cleaning moments, my mind can't help but be drawn back to my early days of helping out around the house with my mother. I learned how to make my own bed fairly early on, taking off the sheets every Saturday for washing and then fitting them back on the bed after they were clean. Mom taught me how to do this and learned a trick from her grandmother or mom; she folded the sheets in methodical order, the same way every time. She then directed me where to place the folded bundle on the bed and in what order to unfold the layers. Every week, I put the origami-like fitted sheet in the middle of the bed, unfolded it partway and unrolled it out across the bottom half of the bed, then unrolled the other folded half toward the head, tucked each fitted part of the sheet around the four corners of the mattress, and proceeded to appropriately lay out the flat sheet. After the flat sheet had been unfolded in its order, I practiced my hospital corners with Mom until I got that just right too. It never came untucked during the week.

With Mom's little method, I was able to make my bed even when I was a tiny child; if she had just handed me a pile of rumpled sheets fresh from the dryer, I would have been much too small to snap each sheet, billowing it out over the bed like an unfurling parachute, like many people do to make their beds. But thanks to her methodically folded sheets, I was able to feel accomplished and confident. Now I just have to make sure I have the method down-pat to teach to Brianna.

Mom also gave me a set of chores to do outside my room, which for most of my life included vacuuming the living room, cleaning the bathroom, and dusting. I didn't mind the vacuuming, although it was a drag to pull all of the pieces of the vacuum out, fit them together, and lug them around the room as I sucked up dirt, and I usually did my bathroom chores first. I've always liked cleaning bathrooms, perhaps because it's easiest to notice the big difference between the dirty "before" and clean "after." But I disliked the dusting, for some reason, as mentioned before, and as a rule Mom would have to ask me around noon on Saturdays if I'd gotten to it yet, and most often I'd reply that I just hadn't had the chance in my busy schedule of cartoon-watching. No matter what was my favorite or least favorite, I felt that I was contributing and seeing results from my efforts.

All of these examples are mundane, routine, "drudgery"- type household tasks. Nothing exciting or special. Nothing I would put on a resume or ask my children to mention in my eulogy someday. But I still get a thrill from having accomplished these everyday chores. I can go to bed at night feeling good that I made a difference in making my own home pleasant and comfortable for my family.

My husband and my children can enjoy what I've done to make our home pretty and clean, and they can participate and feel the same sense of accomplishment. My husband grew up with a solid work ethic and takes pride in his chores around the house (particularly his yard and gardening efforts), and now we can teach our children to feel good about themselves by working. Brianna is feeling good about herself by being my "little helper," feeding Marissa, fetching diapers, or cleaning the bathtub. If I deprived her of doing these little things for me, she wouldn't have the same feelings of worth and involvement.

Everyone needs to feel needed, that they're contributing. Often, it's just the small things that make the difference; no one needs to write a symphony or raise a million dollars for a charity every day (nor is it feasible to do something on a grand scale all the time) to feel they are worth a lot to someone else. I feel needed in my home when I make my house cozy for my family. I feel important when I can cheer up a friend who is feeling down by listening to her on the phone or sending a funny card. I feel happy when I can set the same example for my daughters. I hope I can teach my girls that they are strong, vibrant, lovable, worthwhile creatures, much like my mom did for me. Maybe they *will* write symphonies or find a cure for cancer, but I am sure that neither they nor I would be happier than if they're just making some little difference in our family — and in the human family — every day.

One day recently Brianna reminded me again in a concrete way how anyone can make their mark on the world, even in a small way. The windows of our house were her chalkboard as my tiny teacher spelled out her lesson — quite literally.

Our house is a good forty years old. We've owned it for a few years now at this writing and we've already painted the entire interior, installed three faucets, two toilets and a vanity, replaced the central air-conditioning unit (ouch to the bank account!), and pulled up a bunch of old shrubs and useless trees and so on. We've done a lot more in upkeep and maintenance and the usual odds and ends, so much I really can't remember all that we've tackled anymore. Our next big goal is to replace the windows. These are old and tired. My husband has already re-glazed and painted them to keep them from leaking, but they're just in dire need of complete replacement. There are no screens, so when we open the windows (with a little work) to let in fresh air, the bugs come right along with it. I can't wait to have new, vinyl windows. Another main reason I can tell these windows are old is that moisture condenses on them when the weather provides the right conditions. I know enough about home ownership to realize that condensation is a bad sign. We just need new windows.

So when our windows were fogged up again, Brianna immediately was drawn to the exposed window in my bedroom, where she discovered a wonderful canvas for her particular brand of art. Naturally, as if pulled by an invisible cord, her hand made its way to the clean slate of beaded-up moisture. She wrote a few letters and drew the ubiquitous and requisite smiley face. Pleased with her newfound medium and its results, she turned to me wearing a big smiley face herself.

The urge to write and draw didn't end with a wet window. Faced with the prospect of fresh snow and its virgin white tableau, my daughter immediately tramped around and made footprints and fingerprints in the canvas, creating breakthrough patches of brown-dirt graffiti. She couldn't resist such a perfect medium for art. She had to make her mark.

So it is with all of us. We find we have to make our mark on the world, in whatever form most matches our personality, in whatever medium most closely suits the time, the opportunity, and the message we want to share. I have found I want to make my mark by writing. I want to share what is in my head and in my heart and to know that someone else out there identifies with it and is moved in some way because I've transmitted those thoughts and feelings to paper. I also want to know that my face-to-face interactions with other people have had some positive impact. I want to know that I've somehow managed to put my (bad or good) experiences to some use, to help someone else so they won't have to go through what I did, learning the hard way. I want to know my smile or kind words or gentle encouragement have made a difference. I want to touch and enrich lives.

Everyone makes their mark in different ways. Some have touched millions of lives by their actions or their words; Martin Luther King Jr. changed attitudes, habits and laws by how he acted and what he did, the example he set for people of all colors. Mother Teresa inspired millions with her humble acts of selflessness and generosity. Others have quietly influenced generations by teaching their own brood of children strong values, good manners, kindness, integrity, a love of learning. Though I have no relatives that I know of who have been famous in any way, they have all made their marks. My grandparents' love and personalities will never be forgotten, as I have written about them and share my memories of them with my children. My parents' encouragement and persistence, each in their own ways, have touched me and made me into who I am, and consequently will affect the lives of all I come in contact with. All have made their marks.

Brianna made temporary marks in the snow and in the foggy window, which disappeared as quickly as footprints or castles in the sand washed away by the tide. But I am confident she will make her mark in the world, on those around her, that even as she does now, people in coming years will remember her for her cheerful disposition, ready smile, and bright laughter and speech. She will touch their lives as she touches mine every day.

CHAPTER 14
FROM GIRLS TO GRANDMAS

I had always thought of my mom as one of those people who were natural mothers, and that I had not inherited it. Sure, she had some imperfections and we had our "issues" to work out as I settled into (and continued) adulthood, but I thought that mothering was what she had always planned on, looked forward to, and relished. She was a stay-at-home mom; she married not long before her twenty-eighth birthday (after a fulfilling jaunt as a middle-school English and drama teacher), moved, quit her teaching job, and focused on taking care of me, born shortly before her twenty-ninth birthday, and my two siblings who came later.

I am not assuming that she relished and enjoyed her new vocation just because of outward appearances, what with her decision to be a traditional full-time mother. Rather, I always felt that way because of the quantity and quality of time she spent with me and how she later recounted her experiences raising me as a young child. She seemed to have really savored that time, even the mundane day-to-day tasks.

Over the years, mom told me about all the things she enjoyed watching me do — analyzing ants as a small toddler as we took leisurely strolls around the neighborhood together, listening to me spell out the letters in stop signs and Sears storefronts, and so on. Her own unhappy marriage and eventual divorce, unfulfilled dreams, and status as a single woman with two jobs and not many resources seemed to fall away as she related the tales of those simple, mundane things. Her eyes lit up, her face glowed, she remembered the good times when her children were young. She seemed so thoroughly immersed in motherhood, in watching me grow and learn.

So with this impression of her as a mom, I couldn't help but compare myself as a mom to her. It seemed impossible to me that I would be as happy as she was being "just a mom" because I didn't have that feeling of enchantment at the time I started out on my mothering gig. I never felt like a natural mother. I wasn't in love with the idea of having babies and watching them grow; I didn't glow with the anticipation of it all. I was nervous and unsure of how it would derail my personal goals, my grand plans for my career. Although I felt confident, intellectually and somewhere in my gut, that becoming a mother was an important step for me to take, I felt I was lacking something vital.

As I found out months after taking that giant step into the wild pink yonder, what was lacking was my own firstborn daughter. The collected moments with Brianna have bit by bit given me new and profound insight on how my mother must have felt as a new mom. Within a period of thirteen or fourteen months, she went from single woman and teacher of junior-high students to married woman and mother of a baby girl who would shortly become a bright, curious and sometimes mischievous young child.

Having my daughter, observing her discoveries and watching her personality emerge, has awakened the "natural mother" in me over a period of time and tied me more closely to my own mother. The three of us — all firstborn daughters, strong, fiercely independent, and gregarious — have emerged as links in a chain that binds us through three generations and more.

It was through a new twist she introduced into our bed-time-reading routine one evening that Brianna really brought into focus for me the feeling of that multi-generational link. I had felt its presence before, a sense that some shimmering, near-invisible force was reaching out from around and behind and ahead of us, pulling us females of the family from different time periods on the calendar into some kind of loop that was out of time. The gossamer threads of that force were often just to the side of my direct line of sight, winking and undulating, but at this moment I turned my head, as it were, and saw them directly. I felt as if I were several women at once, inhabiting one body, looking out of the eyes of the girl that physically sat in front of me in the here and now, as well as out of the eyes of a girl about twenty-five years earlier and her mother as well.

"Who is this from?" Brianna began asking as she pulled each book out of the cubby next to her bed. She wants to know who gave her all those books. The answer is usually "This one is from Grandma ... or Mom ... or Grampa ... or Mommy's friend. ..." Sometimes Mommy's memory has faded, and I have no interesting answer. I know I didn't buy the book, but I can't recall who in the world gave us that particular tome at a long-ago baby shower. If I honestly respond, "I don't know," that answer is unacceptable, and Brianna more loudly and insistently repeats the question, "Where is this *from*?!" until I at least lamely answer that it's from "a friend."

I'm not completely sure why she keeps asking me this question lately; it's impossible to peek into the mind of a small child and know for sure their motivations or their wisdom or understanding. My guess is simply that with each book, given to us from her infant days up until the present by friends and relatives, she is reassured that a large number of people love her enough to stock her library. When my mom sent a new book a month or two ago, we read the fresh piece of literature over and over again the moment I took it out of its package, thus turning it into a very familiar, memorized, broken-in favorite. Even though it only took a few minutes to read, and Brianna has a pretty good memory, she continued to ask during every title-page reading where it came from. Even though I knew she knew who had given it to her, I can only guess she found a sense of comfort, almost a postage-paid hug, in being reminded of the loving, grandmotherly origins of the book.

Then a similar question popped up in a different setting. It didn't directly correlate to the multifarious sources of her books, but it came from the same place in her heart. She was making connections to find out where she herself had come from. She asked me, "Does Daddy have a mama?"

Her sweet, logical question broke my heart. Brianna figured out long ago that my mom is her grandma — she has a mommy, I have a mommy. She extended this reasoning to her father and realized no face in her mind matched the "daddy's mom" slot. And it struck me forcefully that she would never have a memory of her own of her paternal grandmother, for my firstborn was only a year old when my husband's mother died.

I knew it would come to this; I just didn't expect to be faced so soon with the holes in her familial recollections. I loved my mother-in-law, Brianna's "Nona," deeply. Two years after her passing, I daily face the emptiness in my heart created by her marked absence, but at least I have a full slate of memories to draw upon. My heart has a hole, but my mind's video library is stocked. It's time to start showing those "videos" to my daughter.

My parents did the same with me, and their parents before them. Every generation passes on its archived memories of loved ones on to the next, so those who provided us and our parents not only with our first breaths but with the foundations of how we would daily take those breaths would be remembered forever, with each new generation.

My mom speaks particularly fondly of her grandfather, a melon farmer. Oddly enough, Mom doesn't like to eat watermelon or cantaloupe (she says they're tasteless), but she remembers visiting him on his farm and learning from him how to pick the most flavorful. She always chooses the best melons for the rest of us, and I like to think I have inherited it from her; perhaps it's in my blood. Armed with my inborn gift and secondhand memories of a farming great-grandfather, a trip to the market is almost a religious experience. I connect with the fruit I handle, feeling whisperings of ancestors gone before guiding my hand and my nose as I select the best.

Perhaps my mother experiences those same feelings as she visits the grocery store. I haven't noticed. But I do observe the faraway look in her eyes, the tear-blurred vision, the choked-up hesitation in her voice as she speaks of her grandfather and his work, his life, their time together. She has a few items left to physically remind her of him — some browned black-and-white photographs, a few trinkets, a beautiful old bedroom set. She was so eager to acquire his four-poster bed and mirrored dresser from her mother, as Grandma moved out of her house and into a small retirement-facility room. Mom prizes this irreplaceable possession as a tangible gift from her long-gone grandfather.

I treasure up my own memories of my grandfather, who died when I was just fifteen. I remember sitting on his lap as a child Brianna's age and telling him he needed to give up smoking (which he did a few years later). I remember count-less hours sitting in the living room with him and Grandma, as an easy-listening radio station on the stereo system provid-ed a generic background throughout the house (Granddad liked it, but it drove my dad nuts). He sat in his recliner, read-ing the newspaper and sometimes watching the sporting news on television, with a set of earphones silently connecting his ear to a portable radio with a TV band. Often, by the time the eleven o'clock newscast was over, Granddad would be asleep in that chair, feet up, mouth slightly open. It was my cue to go to bed, after depositing a non-awakening kiss on the top of his bald forehead. I can almost feel even all these years later the sensation of the smoothness of his shiny skin on my lips, the solid bone underneath, the utter stillness of the late-night household with its background noises of clock ticking and the sounds of slumber from all the filled bedrooms.

My grandfather's work is largely unknown to me; he had a government office job until retirement, leaving me no mem-ories of an agrarian connection to the land. But his beloved post-retirement hobby is my memory's playground. He had an extremely well-equipped workshop in the basement, complete with every tool known to man and then some. The joke went that no one could buy him a gift for his shop for Christmas or a birthday because as soon as a new tool was available, he dashed to the neighborhood do-it-yourself store and bought it himself. One Christmas my mom, throwing up her hands in defeat, decided all she could buy him was a beautiful, expen-sive piece of wood with which he could create a new master-piece.

My grandfather spent a great deal of time in his basement shop. I joined him to observe all of the careful cutting and sanding and finishing work. He allowed my presence and sometimes showed me how to use all of his expensive toys. He made gifts (never for pay) for family and friends and even equipped his church's pews with hymnal holders. One year he made me a beautiful musical jewelry box. He signed the bottom of his creations, including my jewelry box, with a tool fabricated for permanently etching words into wood.

Finding this tool particularly amazing, I asked my grandfather to show me how it worked. How could he get his name into a solid piece of wood? He brought out a castoff square of lumber and his handy-dandy tool and gave me a demonstration. It was like writing on paper with a vigorously vibrating thick pen; it just required a little extra control and concentration. Granddad let me have a spin, and we took turns engraving our names over and over on the small piece of wood. I was so proud of our work that I kept it. A few years after he died, I remembered our efforts that day and searched frantically for that keepsake. Luckily, I never threw out anything as a teenager, so I was able to find my treasure. Now, I display it in my living room with other valuable memorabilia, and anytime I catch a glimpse of that small piece of wood I can fondly recall my grandfather and his beloved hobby. What's more, when Brianna gets tall enough to take notice of the wood and curiosity sparks a question, I can share my memories of my granddad with her, passing on my love of him to my daughter just as my mother has and still does with me.

When it comes to Brianna learning about her grandmother, my husband will share his stories about his mom — obviously, he has many because she was with him for thirty years — and I will share my own perspective of Brianna's sweet Nona. I only knew her for four and a half years, but I loved her instantly and thoroughly.

One thing I can tell Brianna about is the first time I talked with her grandmother, when my husband and I were dating at college, and his family lived a full day's drive away. My husband went home for a weekend for a grad-school interview, and I used his car to drop him off and pick him up from the airport near school. He called me from home the morning he was to fly back to college, allegedly to let me know when his flight was. But I knew better: I already had written down when he was scheduled to come in and was eagerly looking forward to it. I knew my guy was calling because he missed me and because he wanted his family to have a low-key opportunity to "meet" me over the phone lines. I'm sure he spent that weekend talking about his new girlfriend, and they were eager to talk to me. My husband gave me the flight number and its arrival time, and then told me his mom wanted to say hi to me. When he passed the phone to her, I heard a sweet voice from the other end of the line greeting me in a friendly, happy yet shy way. I enjoyed the warm reception from this refined little lady and felt honored that my new beau thought enough of me to introduce us.

I met her in person just a few weeks later, when my husband had another interview and decided to drive out this time. He asked me to accompany him, and since I had never been to San Francisco, I agreed excitedly. I was going to get a free trip to a new and exotic locale, plus enjoy a full weekend on the road with my increasingly serious paramour. I was also going to get to *meet the family.*

My reception was just as warm in person. My mother-in-law-to-be welcomed me as if I were already engaged to her dear son and soon to become part of the family. She introduced me to the Filipino hospitality I grew to appreciate later and to her own foreign background and upbringing. During that long weekend, I spent several hours talking alone with her, standing at the counter in the kitchen or sitting in the living room looking out the window, seemingly out over the brown hills of California far in the distance to the Philippines, and asking questions about her fascinating life, so different from my American roots. I heard about her huge family, her status as the baby of thirteen children raised on a farm in the countryside, and her long, cash-poor immigration to California with her husband and three very small children. I listened raptly. I loved her stories, I loved her humble yet enthusiastic way of telling them, and I loved her.

I can tell Brianna of the encouragement my mother-in-law gave me in her own small way. She was very excited when, just a few days married and only a couple of weeks into my California residency, I got a job at a local newspaper. Not considering herself a writer, she thought my talent and interest in writing was fascinating, perhaps because it was foreign to her or perhaps because it reminded her of her days as a successful and very bright student. She gave me pretty, flowery pens and stationery. She eagerly complied when I asked her for an interview so I could write an article about her and her husband's early experiences and work in our church. I've kept that piece, though it was never published anywhere, and I've kept the box of stationery on which she wrote a message for me: "Hope you can use these stationery and cards in sharing your literary talent and writings. It's great knowing you and a privilege to have you in our family soon. Love, Leticia". She was proud of my unique talents. I'll share this with Brianna.

I'll tell Brianna about how her Nona came to stay with us for several weeks shortly after I gave birth to my first baby. How my generous mother-in-law stayed up during the nights with my wide-awake newborn to allow me to get some extra rest. How she tenderly and happily played with her fourth granddaughter, singing her songs about how she had just come from heaven. My husband caught a fraction of this on videotape; the rest is all in my own collection and will have to be shared from my heart, not on a television screen.

Maybe I'll tell my daughter a little about the occasional friction and misunderstandings, for a little perspective that each of us has our moments that aren't so great. That you don't always get along perfectly even with those you love dearly. I know that will be the case with me and Brianna, as it was true with me and my mom and me and my mother-in-law. She'll know the reality of loving relationships. But she'll also know that no matter what, the good times win out and are never forgotten, and those are what we pass on to our children and their children.

My daughter will hear all of these stories and more. She'll get to know her daddy's mama, even though she can't remember her singing those heavenly songs to her and she can't remember her sweet little voice or four-foot-ten-and-three-quarters stature. She'll get to know my granddad and her grandma's granddad. One day years from now, she'll tell her children the same stories, the fondness palpable in her voice even though all she really knew were pictures and passed-along tales. And her stories about her grandma, and her dad and her mom, will be added to those tales. I only hope she will speak of me with that same love and fondness and wistfulness, wishing that we could have all lived forever in real life and not just in memories, old scraps of wood and notes on stationery boxes.

Don't ever tell a child about an exciting event a day or two, and especially not more than three days, in the future (since even "tomorrow" is a pretty foreign concept). You'll hear about it constantly until the event actually comes to pass.

I've made the mistake — or perhaps it's not a mistake — of telling Brianna we're going to Grandma's in, say, four days. Most recently was Christmastime. I was excited about it myself and it bubbled over to my conversations with Brianna. After I mentioned that we'd be going to see Grandma for Christmas, every time we got in the car, approached the car, or even saw the car (as it happens, Brianna can see our car in the carport through the window merely inches from the head of her bed), she said, "Are we going to Grandma's now?" If I said we were going somewhere else, she seemed to try to restrain herself from appearing disappointed. One day as we arrived home from another of our usual destinations (the gym or the store) and I eased our car to a stop in the carport, she indignantly demanded, "Hey! This isn't Grandma's! Don't stop!"

There's just something about Grandma's. For Brianna maybe the excitement is in the variety, the change of pace from home and the boring old amusements here. My mom has a bookshelf in her living room half-filled with toys (mainly trucks and motorcycles and the like) my nephew plays with — or, to be more accurate, throws around — when he's visiting, and books that are a little more gender-neutral, such as "My B Book" and "My A Book" (but, conspicuously, not any of the other alphabet), a few Dr. Seuss offerings and some elementary picture books. I usually read to her at naptime and bedtimes, not that I'm against reading any other time, but the moment we walk in the door, Brianna hops into my mom's lap and drafts her into reading the entire collection.

In the way of film diversion, *Pinocchio* rests on the top shelf, which Brianna wears out during our sojourns at Grandma's because our reasonably modest Disney collection excludes the little wooden boy. When we leave my mom's house, it takes a few days to exorcise "I Got No Strings" from dancing its little jig around my mental soundtrack (aaack! I shouldn't have mentioned that — it's in my head again). I'm just glad Mom doesn't own *Annie* because hearing "Tomorrow" chirping obnoxiously in my brain for days would be worse than enduring the Chinese water torture.

Or perhaps the attraction of Grandma's is the lure of the computer, which my nephew calls the "pooter." Don't get me wrong, we have one at home, but I've steadfastly kept it off-limits for Brianna. One, I don't want her to screw up a thousand-dollar piece of complex equipment, since it's easy enough for me to do that on my own; and two, I have a hard enough time prying my husband's game-playing fingers off the mouse so I can use the gadget to write and send e-mails. I've been reticent to add a three-year-old's small but incredibly strong fingers to the mix. There are only so many hours in the day!

At Grandma's, however, Brianna is welcome almost any time (unless my husband is with us and has managed to take turns with my mom to play Free Cell) to sit at the controls like a big girl, piecing together puzzles and guiding cute animated pirate stories with quick, deft swishes of the mouse. After a few visits (frankly, after just a few minutes of screen time on her first crack at the magic machine), Brianna is able to do everything herself. She calls for "help" but is only doing so to get Mom or Grandma to *ooh* and *aahh* over her mastery of the games.

Perhaps Brianna loves Grandma's house so much because of the food or the different bed. She gets pancakes and sausage on demand on a different plate than she has at home. For a while, she slept in Grandma's king-size waterbed, but now she has her very own futon, both of which are more exotic and fascinating than her standard twin-size at home.

I remember getting to eat special food at my grandmother's home when I was Brianna's age. For some reason, cantaloupe, alphabet soup and Nilla wafers come to mind. I'm sure my grandma fed me more than that, but the brain has a way of choosing particular slices of time to recall over others. In my head, a search for "food at Grandma's" always turns up the same entry at the top of the list. When I think back on later years when I was older, a more complete list springs up, like seedless white grapes ready in a bowl when we arrived in summertimes and Grandma's special-recipe banana pudding the first night after dinner. She also invariably made fruit salads with refreshing frozen, straight-from-Hawaii pineapple and strawberries. Homemade apple jelly was on hand for toast, and refried beans were pulled from the deep freezer in the basement to be defrosted for me to eat with the omnipresent corn chips, easily available in the cabinet next to the kitchen table. Orange Crush in sixteen-ounce bottles (a real treat since my parents only let us drink soda once a week or so) rested in six-packs on the garage floor just outside the kitchen door, and breakfasts could range from Rice Krispies to eggs and sausage, another treat because my mom usually just had bacon in our refrigerator when I was growing up. Funny how she now has sausage all the time when we visit.

Depending on how many relatives were visiting at once, I slept different places. If I was alone on a visit, I slept in the lush green-carpeted room furnished with my mom's granddad's prized four-poster bed and matching mirrored dresser. I lay there at night and heard just peace and quiet, occasionally broken by an ambulance siren in the distance. I felt very special and grown-up to sleep in that room. If the entire family was gathered for a holiday, I was relegated to the basement laundry room, where a cot was set up for me in the corner, which I made private and snazzy by hanging a sheet on the clothesline in the middle of the room, effectively creating a separate haven for myself.

I enjoyed that laundry room and its privacy, with the clock radio above the old stove, available to play tinny music from the many radio stations there in the big city, and the closeted toilet close at hand. I liked the laundry chute located to the left of my cot; it connected to the bathroom upstairs and was the perfect way to communicate with anyone in the main part of the house. If it was mealtime, I was easily reachable. With my siblings and cousins sharing the big living room down-stairs, I was the privileged oldest grandchild sleeping alone in that little room.

I concede that my grandparents had few toys or amuse-ments in their home, nothing geared particularly for visiting grandchildren. We could play cards with Grandma or watch baseball games or work in the shop with Granddad; I could leaf through stacks of old *Life* magazines or try in vain to deposit a little metal ball in a round hole by maneuvering a pair of parallel metal poles. Neither of these activities held my attention for long, so the main allure of the grandparents' house was the other aforementioned treats. But Orange Crush or banana pudding aside, the quiet home was primarily a con-stant in my life, a place I could count on as a steady, secure retreat, virtually unchanged every time I visited.

Through twenty-plus years of moving around, probably fifteen different houses and not as many cities and states, I knew I had the same house to visit every summer and holiday. My grandparents moved there when I was about five years old, and Grandma stayed there past my grandfather's death and on until I was twenty-seven, when she moved into a retirement facility. The house was always the same, the same cookies kept in the cold garage at Christmas, the same bed, the same ticking of the grandfather clock in the living room.

My mom now has that grandfather clock. It ticks like a metronome in her living room, transplanted from my grandparents' constant living room. I think that front room was my favorite part of the house; it was warm and sunny during the day, with light pouring in through the large front windows, and cozy and close in the evenings. The same furniture, kept in perfect condition for years, as I remember it, adorned the room, and three or more lamps made little pools of light at night, perfect for quiet reading. I knew that I wanted to have a living room just like that, not lit by one large, almost impersonal, overhead light, but bathed in cozy clusters of bulbs softened by beige lampshades.

In the evenings as I stayed up late in that room with my grandparents, those lamps made secure little pockets, engulfing us each in a personal but not isolated world of reading or TV-watching. My grandmother worked crossword puzzles sitting in one armchair next to a lamp, relaxed enough to nod off while still clutching her pencil and daily newspaper, glasses perched on the end of her nose. My grandfather listened to his baseball games or nightly news through his earphones and watched a mute television set, kicked back in his recliner. I enjoyed their ever-present, assuring company as I would read my stash of books brought from home.

During all this, the clock ticked on, the pendulum swaying back and forth, lulling us and saying "All is well, all is well" over and over again. Often it was past eleven or eleven-thirty, much later than my usual bedtime, when I would glance at that clock's face and the drowsy faces of my grandparents and note that once again it was time to retire to either my concrete-floored laundry room hideout or my green-carpeted, plush four-poster retreat. As I lay in the upstairs room, I could still hear the metronome sound clicking on.

The rooms with their beds and the kitchen and garage with their food offerings have all been stripped of their personalities and the almost-living inhabitants redistributed to other homes. A few reside in my grandma's little studio, which looks now just like her house but in miniature. Most are in my aunt and uncle's home and in my mom's house. A few relics have found their way to my home. I have Grandma's good china and a few odds and ends, mostly in a pretty little china cabinet I indulged in specifically to house these treasures. I can't say at this stage of my life that I have a great deal of nice, quality furniture, but I found a gem to hold my memories of my grandparents' house. Every time I sit down to eat at my old, hand-me-down table complete with cheap, cast-off, mismatched chairs, I can gaze into the beautiful cabinet and enjoy being reminded of the holiday meals we ate off that china and the other times I spent in that house that is now just a memory for me.

One of the treasures I enjoy the most is a small, plain music box with a faded, now two-color illustration of a little boy with a puppy. The picture on top means little to me; I don't usually think of the box's appearance when it comes to mind. What stirs up deeply embedded, ancient memories of my childhood is the sound the box makes when I open the top. Inside is a simple metal comb that clicks off a melody when each prong is struck by a Braille-like dot on a rotating cylinder. The tune that floats hesitatingly and methodically from the box is that of "The Sound of Music." The cylinder's circumference is too small to play more than a few phrases of the song; since it cannot play the entire tune, I am always left with a sense that it has never ended. It just goes on and on, beginning to middle and over again. When I was Brianna's age, my grandmother wouldn't let me play with the box without supervision; she didn't want me to carelessly break the wind-up mechanism. As I grew older, she allowed me more freedom to pick up the box whenever I wanted and carefully wind it and set off the music by lifting the lid. I listened to it countless times as I grew older.

When she was sorting out all her belongings and distributing them to posterity, Grandma gave me the box and said, "I know you like this, so you can have it. I don't know why you like it so much; it's not worth anything, but here it is. It's yours." I was ecstatic. I enjoy having the expensive china but the little music box that probably cost almost nothing when it was new is the most precious gift she has passed on to me. I can open the box anytime I want now and listen to it rattle off its tune, never ending. It goes on and on and I expect it will as I allow Brianna and her posterity someday to lift the lid and hear the tinny melody plinked out note by note.

The box is precious to me because it brings out firmly entwined, multilayered memories of my childhood and young adulthood, each moment spent at the special retreat known as Grandma's house. Its notes take me back in time, as if everything still remains the way it was and some other family has not taken over and completely redecorated my grandparents' home. I can sit in the living room with my grandmother doing her crossword puzzle, back when she didn't need her eyeglasses all the time, and my now-gone grandfather dozing in his recliner with earphones in his ears. I can feel the tranquility and the warmth of that comfortable, reassuring cocoon, a place of contentment and love. Most of all, I can remember the wonderful loved ones who lived there and sat in that room with me. I will always know that they love me and I love them.

The warmth of the lamps rests in my heart and diffuses itself through my being.

Perhaps that's really the main reason Brianna loves to go to Grandma's: everyone she loves is there. Her grandma has that special love for her, and the things she has are just symbols, extensions, and reminders of that love. Her mom is there too, making a bridge to the familiarity of home. The grandfather clock ticks off its dependable seconds, the pendulum swinging slowly back and forth in a different grandmother's living room. As I sit there in my mother's house, I have some of the old retreat to enjoy, faint whisperings of my grandmother's living room, the same feelings. Someday Brianna will have those same memories. We will both share that heritage and pass it on to our posterity, a reminder that the simple comforts of a loved one's home are always reminders that we are special to them and always will be loved. The heritage is there, in a clock or a music box, whether the loved one is still around or has long since passed on. The symbols we will pass on to our children and children's children to forever remind them and provide that retreat of love, just as my grandmother gave her clock and her music box to her daughter and granddaughter.

A universal bit of wisdom passed down from parent to child is that of retribution: "I can't wait till *you* have kids." My sister was particularly hard-hit by my mom's desire to see some payback: she was known as the wildest child and seemed to get into trouble left and right. As an infant, she woke up my mother consistently through the nights for probably her first couple of years. After that phase passed, she started wandering off unattended, forcing my mother to conduct countless frantic searches for her wayward, curious toddler. I remember trips to Kmart punctuated by announcements over the loudspeaker telling my sister to meet Mom at the front of the store, visits to amusement parks interrupted by her astonishing knack for breaking free from parental control. The list could go on for pages, but I'll spare her the embarrassment.

For my part, I heard repeated tales of my adventures as a toddler — the two most famous including my stirring eggs into the living room carpet with a wooden spoon, just like Mom did with the eggs for the bread; and my agile climbs up small shelves to topple laundry detergent in a huge cloud of spring-fresh powder from the top shelf all the way to the floor below. Mom always marveled about my fingers' and toes' amazing ability to find the tiniest foothold on a very narrow ledge. I'm sure she wasn't as appreciative of my skills at the time I created huge messes in her house.

I imagine she has waited all these years to hear me recount similar tales of woe about the exploits of my own children. I know she has waited years for my sister to experience payback from her energetic young boy. Even as she empathizes and shakes her head with our small frustrations, she also laughs a little (or a lot) and revels in the fact that her time for dealing with these difficulties is past, and that the time has come for her former terrors to be terrorized a little (or a lot) themselves. Justice has been served, the circle has been completed. Ha! Ha-ha-ha.

I haven't talked much to Grandma about what Mom did as a child. Maybe I should start doing some official interviewing and taping with my grandmother. One tale I have heard has actually come straight from the source, not from her mother. Mom said that every Christmas she found the presents, either prior to their being placed under the tree, or after, and stealthily opened them by peeling off tape and carefully removing the contents from the packaging. After getting a good look at what had been given to her, she then just as carefully replaced the wrapping paper and tape as she had found them. No one was ever the wiser. Grandma said she didn't know until Mom told her. Quite a good trick, I may say, and one I never attempted or even thought of. And there must be more. I know Mom's relatively minor experiences with my eggs and Ivory Snow soap all over the laundry room were but trivial payback for her own exploits.

So what goes around comes around in parenting. This law of the familial jungle is true in matters of frustration and enjoyment alike. It is a constant in funny behavioral quirks as well as the big and little manifestations of DNA. Motherhood is a sacred inheritance passed down through the generations.

On the physical side of the equation, I always thought it was funny that my mom and I both had lots of moles (my dermatologist says they're really just freckles, but we always called our spots moles) all over our bodies, on our faces, arms, and legs. Eerily enough, she and I both sport triangle-shaped constellations of moles on our right forearms. The little Bermuda triangles, as I refer to them, are in the same location on both of our arms, just below the inside of our elbows, and in a very similar grouping. More little moles are popping out on Brianna's skin, and I will be curious to see if she will join us in our Bermuda triangles.

My mom also has very bad knees. For years, I've winced as I heard her joints crack and pop as she's moved or even sat still. Oftentimes, I would be sitting on her lap, reading a book or just snuggling, when one of her legs would suddenly buck up like a rider-fettered bull, of its own accord, as if her knee had been struck with a reflex-testing mallet, sending me, the rider, to one side or the other. She would wince and apologize, saying there was nothing she could do about it. Now, before I've even hit the age of thirty, my knees are cracking and popping like corn dancing around in a hot oiled pan (or microwave), and I know I'm destined for the same fate. My husband tells me I should take care of my knees now; I'm already thinking about taking some of that glucosamine/chondroitin. It's expensive and I'm young still, so I continue to put it off. But the popcorn sound won't go away, in my knees or my mom's.

Our legs and hands are also alike, not just in how they behave or how they sound or in how they're ornamented, but in their shape. My mom, bless her heart, has a little pocket on each side of her outer thighs, that has been passed on to me and my sister (even my taller, more willowy sibling has little pockets on her thin, amazing gams). No matter how I exercise and do leg lifts and weights, those bags won't go away. They may look diminished and almost disappear, but I can still feel the reality of their presence. I bet even liposuction wouldn't take care of those cellulite ovals. They're an inescapable inheritance. I think Mom said all the women in her family had them. That's comforting. I can already see their inevitable beginnings in the cute, tiny little legs of my daughter. She's gonna have 'em too.

Our hands are the same. Our hands and fingers are small, with fairly short but not stubby fingers. They're fairly well-proportioned but just not long and slender and perfect for piano-playing. I've never been able to go much beyond a solid eighth on the keyboard. That's a reality I'm OK with; I don't aspire to be a concert pianist, and my anatomy and training are quite adequate for weekly church playing. I'll never be a lotion or nail polish model either, but I think I have fairly cute hands.

Mom passed on at least part of her fingernails to me too. Her fingernails are quite distinctive: they're flat and don't curve under at the tips. They just go straight out. Needless to say, she's kept them fairly short most of her life and has largely avoided fingernail polish. My nails aren't as flat as hers, thanks to the influence of my father's DNA, but they don't gracefully curve under at the tips either, and my pinkie nails are both just like Mom's. They're flat and actually angle up at the tips instead of under. The first thing I noticed when my first daughter was born was her fingers. Even though she was only seven pounds, with tiny everything, I could see her hands were shaped just like mine, fingernails included in the bargain. It was strange to see miniature versions of hands I'd been staring at and using for twenty-six years. After all, your hands are almost always right in front of you, readily available for examination (why else would the phrase "I know it like the back of my hand" exist?). I had given my small hands and small but proportioned fingers, along with those nails, right to my oldest daughter. That was also the first thing I noticed when I gave birth to my second daughter: her hands and fingernails were nothing like mine. I was just as amazed. It was fascinating to peer closely at her tiny fingers and see that she had inherited my mother-in-law's curved-under fingernails. Wow! She got a little lucky there. Nail polish would look much better on her hands.

Strange behavioral similarities have popped up in me and my daughters, things I can't explain by either nurture or nature. My mom occasionally smiled to herself when she happened to catch me drinking a cup of juice or water. She explained that even as a teenager or adult I drank just as I did as a toddler: I took a long gulp and breathed in deeply and quickly, as if coming up for air, before going for the next long swig. She didn't know why I did that but here I was still drinking the same way. Then when my first daughter started drinking out of a cup, my mom observed her doing the same thing: drinking as much as possible in one long continuous gulp, then breathing in desperately before another go-round. It was so obvious and noticeable to my mom that she laughed again and couldn't believe I had somehow passed it on to my daughter.

Now my husband has learned to notice our drinking habits, making astonished and amused comments whenever she and I or now my second daughter come up for air between sips. I myself find it amusing and uncanny. Surely I didn't *teach* my daughters to drink that way, and surely it's not something passed along in my genes. If it were, where did I get it from? Some great-great-grandmother a few generations back? It's a very curious phenomenon.

So watching my daughters, their physical traits and funny habits, has been very entertaining, to say the least, and almost an experience in familial déjà vu, a *Freaky Friday*-type switching of bodies and times. My mother remarked to me recently on a visit that she had been struck with the feeling that she was her mother and I was her, when she was a young mother as I am now. She was starting to get the feeling of what it was like to be her mom, watching her dealing with a young daughter and all of its associated joys and frustrations.

In turn, I've begun to realize the past few years how my mother felt when I was a child. She's told me so many stories over the years of how it was to watch me grow and learn. She told me sometimes of my exploits, of course, about the things I did that made her a little crazy, in typical payback parenting style, but more frequently observed to me, nostalgically, how much fun she had being a mother. She was fascinated by *my* fascination with the ants on the sidewalk. She thrilled at the everyday experiences, at each new milestone I reached. She loved to read to me, to start hearing me read back to her, to recognize "stop" on a red octagonal road sign or "Sears" on a department store.

My mom was there for all the little mundane things I did, and in her memories of those days, she seemed to revel in my accomplishments and in my discoveries, milestones that will never show up on a résumé or be rewarded with a prize. Having been a junior-high teacher and drama coach for a number of years, she didn't seem to miss the accolades, the gifts of yellow roses and the applause for a job well done on a play. She seemed to derive great pleasure and satisfaction from knowing she was raising a happy, growing child. Even now when she recalls those days a generation ago, her eyes light up and her face and voice take on a peculiar tone and look, one of happiness and longing and bittersweet remembrance.

I'm just starting to understand that now, and I am recognizing those same sounds resonating in my voice when I talk about my daughters and the feelings of pride and gratitude that I get to be around for what they do. I *really* do miss the pats on the back from co-workers, the paychecks, the instant rewards for a job well done. But I understand now what it's like to see my own sweet little child take her wobbly first steps or to call out for me or read to me. I know the pleasure inherent in just watching her face, intent on a project, brows furrowed slightly, lips pursed, tongue out a little, her whole body showing satisfied concentration. I know what it's like to hear her figure out words or recognize letters from her name in signs on the street. I am standing in the shoes of my mom twenty years ago and knowing what it's like to watch myself as a child. The circle is coming around to me and it's my turn to be the mom.

Just as I see that my daughter inherited my moles and my pouchy thighs and my fingernails, I know she will inherit the birthright of mother, no matter what else she wants to do with her life. She will stand and watch her child, imagining what it's like to be me. She may miss her doctoring or her lawyering or her writing (heaven forbid!), and most likely she will chafe at the indignities and pains of the transition from single gal to mother of young children, just like I did, but she will finally understand what I will have been telling her for years: how much I enjoyed all the accumulated moments being her mom. How I enjoyed watching her pick little weeds to present to me as beautiful bouquets, how my heart swelled when I watched her sleep, how I got so excited when she figured out on her own how to write her name. One day she'll tell me she understands what it was like to be me and the cycle will go on.

ACKNOWLEDGEMENTS

I cannot have written this book or put it out there for anyone else to read had it not been for the support of a number of people, to whom I am indebted. First, my daughter Brianna was the inspiration for this book. She is now six years older than when I first began jotting down ideas, and is much more grown-up, but is still just as amazing and inspiring as she was at age three.

Next, my husband, Marcelino Lim Jr., always, always allowed me to hole myself up at the computer whenever the muse compelled me to turn my notes into prose, while he kept our daughters company (usually in front of the TV). He has been behind me every step of the way, doing more than his share, being a rare man and husband indeed.

I thank all those who have gone before me, especially my mother, Carol Cromer, and my father, Ralph Carmode, who didn't spare any love or time on their children. They taught me so much and always encouraged me as I explored my interests. They knew not just the meaning of "quality time," but also of "quantity time." In my memories, we always had all the space and time in the world.

To the parents and grandparents of each of my parents, thank you for what you did to allow them, and me, and my children, to be here. My grandmother Helen Cromer is the only one still living, able to see these words in print; how I wish my grandfather Arthur Boyce Cromer could see them as well. My uncle, Ken Cromer, is not just a library director but someone whose opinion I value. I appreciate his faith in my writing; it has been a boost.

To the teachers who made such an impression upon me

through the years, particularly those who went out of their way to allow me to learn on my own, thank you. I especially thank Lisa Polivick for reading my manuscript and giving her valuable input and support.

My dear friends have made it possible for me to hold on to enough sanity to continue parenting and writing. They are truly life savers. Sarah Crawford is like a sister, a strong, warm and fun person remarkably tuned in to what I need. Suzanne Condie Lambert is my friend still in the business, and an incredibly sharp writer and editor.

My Tuesday night book club is a fantastic group of women, smart, well-read and fun as all get-out. They have always been enthusiastic in all their support of me and my work. Thanks especially to Lesley Cunningham and Ann Summers, who have read my manuscript and given input at various stages, as well as everyone else: Donnie DiValentin, Cathy Earle, Callie McDonald, Hilda Mundy, Jennifer Orcutt, Trish Roberts and Lisa Stefanov. I wish we could meet every day.

Love to all my family — my children, siblings, extended family, and in-laws. The bonds we share are what life is all about.